Contents

Acknowledgements

All the photographs in this book have been selected from Evelyn Dove's private collection, now in the possession of Stephen Bourne, with the exception of the following:
Frank Dove at Cranleigh School (1910) courtesy of Cranleigh School Archives
Evelyn Dove at BBC microphone and Evelyn Dove and Edric Connor at BBC microphone (both 1945) courtesy of the BBC Photograph Library

Special thanks go to the following for their help with this book:
David Hankin for digitally restoring most of Evelyn Dove's photographs (www.davidhankin.com)

Martin Williamson, Cranleigh School Archivist, for providing additional information about Frank Dove's time at the school (1910–1915)
Lesley Daniel, Library Assistant at the Royal Academy of Music, for providing additional information about Evelyn Dove's time at the Academy (1917–1919)
BBC Written Archives
Iain Cameron Williams
Christopher Ginnett
Jeffrey Green (www.jeffreygreen.co.uk)
Keith Howes
Linda Hull
Molly Hull
Howard Rye

Author's Note

In *Evelyn Dove – Britain's Black Cabaret Queen* the terms "black" and "African Caribbean" refer to Caribbean and British people of African origin. Other terms, such as "West Indian", "negro" and "coloured" are used in their historical context, usually before the 1960s and 1970s, the decades in which the term "black" came into acceptable use.

Though every care has been taken, if, through inadvertence or failure to trace the present owners, I have included any copyright material without acknowledgement or permission, I offer my apologies to all concerned.

EVELYN DOVE

BRITAIN'S BLACK CABARET QUEEN

STEPHEN BOURNE

JACARANDA

This edition first published in Great Britain 2016 by
Jacaranda Books Art Music Ltd
Unit 304 Metal Box Factory
30 Great Guildford Street
London SE1 0HS

www.jacarandabooksartmusic.co.uk

A CIP catalogue record for this book is available from the British
Library

ISBN: 978-1-909762-35-0

Cover design by Jeremy Hopes

Book design and typesetting by Head & Heart Publishing Services
www.headandheartpublishingservices.com

Printed and bound in Great Britain by Zenith Media, Wales

This book is dedicated to Isabelle Lucas (1927–1997)

Introduction

Evelyn Dove was a trailblazer. She was the first black female singer on BBC Radio and the first black British female singer to cross the North Atlantic and work in America, a quarter of a century before Shirley Bassey. In 1946 she was the first black woman to have her own popular music series on British television.

Evelyn Dove was one of Britain's most versatile singers. She was equally at home with spirituals, sentimental ballads and emotional torch songs. Throughout the Second World War, on BBC Radio, Evelyn enjoyed the same national recognition as the "Forces Sweetheart" Vera Lynn, who popularised such songs as "We'll Meet Again" and "The White Cliffs of Dover". Like Vera, Evelyn was regularly employed by the BBC as a radio vocalist; she sang in a wide variety of programmes and shone a light to listeners throughout the dark, terrifying days of the war. Before the war, Evelyn had been one of the true pioneers of the booming cabaret age in the 1920s and 1930s. She thrilled audiences around the world, a black British diva who courted admirers and fans wherever she performed. Her mesmerising movie star looks, grace and glamour captivated those in her presence.

Evelyn Dove's career reads like the stuff of soap operas and it would go from strength to strength in the 1930s. She was a young adventuress who refused to be constrained by her race and English middle-class background. The public and press couldn't get enough of this rising star who, at the height of her fame, replaced Josephine Baker as the star attraction in a revue at the Casino de Paris. In 1935, amidst a frenzy of public interest, she arrived in New York to appear in cabaret at the famous nightclub Connie's Inn. This rivalled the Cotton Club as a showcase for top black talent. Her travels then took her to Bombay (now Mumbai), India where her cabaret act was greeted with applause by wealthy white colonials. It was here that a local journalist enthused: "She is superb. Face and figure, voice and melody. She has everything, has Evelyn Dove. You see her and you hear her sing and you are taken back to a front row seat watching 'Blackbirds'. Or the Cotton Club or Connie's Inn. Or just anywhere in New York or Paris between midnight and the milkman." When the same journalist reviewed her opening night, he said: "Evelyn Dove didn't get just the big hand. She got an ovation, a roaring welcome that must have sent all the fish scuttling in terror out of the harbour just outside."

Evelyn's extraordinary career was one of many highs and lows. As a contralto trained at the Royal Academy of Music, Evelyn hoped for a career on the concert platform, or as an opera singer, but for a black singer of her generation the world of jazz and cabaret was more welcoming. With the threat of a Nazi invasion over Europe, Evelyn faced restrictions on travelling abroad, but when the Second World War broke out in 1939, the BBC welcomed her. The warmth and sincerity in Evelyn's singing appealed to the British public who found themselves under threat from Hitler and the Nazis. After the war, Evelyn enjoyed television stardom as one of the BBC's foremost star personalities of the new medium.

Evelyn was the first black British woman to make an impression in the world of entertainment, as a singer and as a star of revue, variety theatres, cabaret and the BBC. She ventured far and wide, to Europe, India and America, but there were limitations. The world was not ready for a black British woman to make a success in show business on a grand, international scale, or to conquer America. This would not happen until Shirley Bassey, the Welsh chart topper, was catapulted to fame in the late 1950s. Among Evelyn's possessions is a faded newspaper cutting from the 1950s, announcing Shirley Bassey as a rising new star. Someone had sent it to Evelyn and written in the margin, "Do you know this person?" During her lifetime, Evelyn could only have dreamed of the success that Shirley aspired to and achieved, and conquering America.

I didn't become aware of Evelyn's existence until the 1980s. I met her friend, Isabelle Lucas, for the first time in 1989 and began to learn more about Evelyn thanks to her. Isabelle invited me to her beautiful home in Kingston upon Thames, Surrey to interview her about her acting and singing career for a project I was working on. When she took me into her living room, I was immediately struck by a large and impressive portrait of Evelyn on her wall. "Oh," I exclaimed. "That's Evelyn Dove!" Isabelle reacted with enthusiasm, "You've heard of Evelyn?" She was surprised when I nodded and, before we started the interview, we spent an hour talking about the forgotten star. Isabelle explained that Evelyn had been admitted to a nursing home some years ago and had passed away in 1987. In spite of her stardom, there had been no obituaries for Evelyn, not even in *The Stage* newspaper. Isabelle told me that after the funeral she returned to the nursing home to collect Evelyn's possessions and was shocked and upset to discover the trunks containing Evelyn's beautiful stage costumes had been thrown away, but thankfully a small trunk had been saved and was given to Isabelle. In great excitement Isabelle showed me the contents of the small trunk. It included Evelyn's scrapbook, about sixty photographs, some music sheets, theatre programmes, a couple of scripts from stage plays she had acted in, a few postcards and some magazines in which she had featured, including a 1939 edition of *Radio Pictorial.*

The photographs dated from her childhood in the Edwardian era to the 1960s. There was a mixture of professional portraits, and several beautiful shots of her at the BBC in the 1940s. There were private snapshots, including some taken abroad on her travels in Europe and India. It was fascinating to look at these photographs and the changing styles in her dress and stage costumes. Evelyn had taste and in her heyday—the 1930s and 1940s—her incredible beauty and glamour shone through.

I longed to know more about Evelyn. Isabelle explained that Evelyn had enjoyed a long and successful career, but it hadn't been without ups and downs. Isabelle and I became friends and she was an invaluable source of information about Evelyn.

Not long after befriending Isabelle I contacted Hugh Palmer, who owned a vast collection of 78rpm recordings. He confirmed that he had some of Evelyn's. She hadn't made many recordings, but Hugh kindly transferred what he had onto a cassette and it was wonderful to hear the voice of this gifted contralto singing popular tunes of the 1930s such as Cole Porter's "My Heart Belongs to Daddy", Judy Garland's 'theme song', "Over the Rainbow" and one of my favourite songs, Richard Rodgers and Lorenz Hart's "Where or When".

Regrettably the BBC had not saved any of Evelyn's numerous appearances on radio, most of which had dated from the 1940s. Immediately I sent a copy of the cassette to Isabelle who wrote back to me:

Thank you so much for your letter and the tape of Evelyn Dove. I do agree she had a lovely voice. Yes, the recordings are lovely. Such a wonderful souvenir. I have some pieces of music which she used in her cabaret act. I don't think I ever heard her actually sing by herself, so I hadn't a chance to judge. I'm surprised there are no recordings of her left in the BBC Radio archives of the '40s period. I don't really know why her reputation faded.

Evelyn's reputation may have faded, but I was determined to find out as much as I could about this grand and brilliant lady.

From the 1920s to the 1930s her star shone brightly. Audiences adored her, and she rivalled some of the now better known black singers and entertainers of that time, such as Josephine Baker, Adelaide Hall and Elisabeth Welch. This was no mean feat for a black *British* artiste, but they all had something in common. They were among the first black women in the entertainment world to break away from the stereotype of the bandana-wearing Mammy of the Southern plantation. Their travels to Europe, especially Paris, opened up new worlds to them, worlds in which they could express themselves away from the shadow of American racism.

In Paris Josephine Baker became a major star and, though she began in the 1920s by taking off her clothes and conforming to French audience's view of her as an exotic savage, in the 1930s she transformed herself into a beautiful and glamorous woman of the world.

Paris also transformed Elisabeth Welch who, when she began singing in cabaret there in 1930 at a famous nightclub called Chez Florence, found herself at the centre of a world inhabited by the rich and famous. She later recalled:

I watched them all, watched their elegance, their poise, how they walked in their beautiful gowns, how they talked, drank and smoked. When I bought my first pair of eyelashes I thought I was Josephine Baker because they were long. I did some extra blinking to let the audience see those! I wanted to be at ease and as elegant as the beautiful women who came into Chez Florence, to move with grace and assurance as well as sing.

Evelyn was also working in Europe at this time, and transforming herself in the same way as Elisabeth, thus creating a glamorous stage persona, far removed from the Mammy or exotic savage. Evelyn carried this persona right through the 1930s and 1940s, but in the 1950s her star began to fade.

Isabelle Lucas became my main source of information but, with the exceptions of Adelaide Hall and Elisabeth Welch, others who worked with her that I spoke to only vaguely recalled Evelyn. However, when I mentioned her name to some older members of the British public who had lived through the Second World War, her name *was* remembered. My father, who was a child in London in the war years, recalled listening to her singing on the "wireless" and he said she had a lovely voice. I also had difficulty in locating members of Evelyn's family, though eventually I did find one of her nieces.

Another problem I faced was Evelyn's absence from published histories of British music and popular entertainment. When I was growing up in the 1970s there weren't that many books around about black British history and next to nothing about black British singers and entertainers. They had been practically airbrushed. I found plenty of material about African American entertainers and jazz musicians. By the age of sixteen I had read books about Dorothy Dandridge, Sammy Davis Jr, Paul Robeson, Duke Ellington and many others.

Unsurprisingly it was Evelyn's African American counterparts who I was drawn to when I was a teenager.

Growing up in London, I was aware that we had two expatriate African American singers living here: Adelaide Hall and Elisabeth Welch. Both of them had known and worked with Evelyn. Back in the 1920s Adelaide and Elisabeth had started out in black Broadway shows and one of them, *Blackbirds of 1928*, had brought them to Paris for an engagement at the

Moulin Rouge. In the 1930s they made London their home and, in 1982, I saw Elisabeth for the first time in concert at the Riverside Studios in Hammersmith. Later that year she invited me to her home in Knightsbridge and we became friends. In 2005, two years after she passed away at the age of ninety-nine, I published her biography, *Elisabeth Welch – Soft Lights and Sweet Music.*

I saw Adelaide in concert for the first time in 1983 and befriended her two years later after interviewing her for *The Voice* newspaper. In 1989 I worked as a consultant on *Sophisticated Lady*, Channel 4's documentary film about her life. To commemorate the centenary of Adelaide's birth in 2001, I published a modest biography, *Sophisticated Lady – A Celebration of Adelaide Hall.* I feel privileged to have befriended Adelaide and Elisabeth, and to have seen them on stage and in their beautiful London homes. I learned much about their lives, careers and the people they worked with throughout their long and illustrious careers.

From Adelaide and Elisabeth I learned a few things about Evelyn Dove. Adelaide had worked with her in the 1920s and again on BBC Television just after the Second World War. Elisabeth had been featured with Evelyn in a popular BBC Radio series called *Rhapsody in Black* (1940) and, thereafter, their paths occasionally crossed. Adelaide and Elisabeth continued working until they were in their nineties. In 1991 Adelaide's ninetieth birthday was celebrated with an all-star concert at the Royal Festival Hall. The following year Elisabeth's career was celebrated with an all-star concert at the Lyric Theatre in London's West End. Adelaide remained active until almost the end of her life. She passed away in 1993. At the age of ninety, Elisabeth retired to Denville Hall where she lived quietly and happily for the remaining years of her life. Elisabeth passed away in 2003. Numerous tributes and obituaries about the two women were published in the press. Adelaide was given an emotional memorial service at the Actor's Church in London's Covent Garden which I attended.

When Evelyn died in a nursing home in 1987, there were no obituaries. No memorial services attended by the elite of Britain's show business. It was a sad situation. Among Evelyn's possessions in old theatrical trunks were her beautiful stage costumes which she had kept right up until the end. These exquisite creations had made her one of the most glamorous entertainers of her time. Life had dealt Evelyn a bitter, cruel blow yet she was determined that something would survive of her fascinating and turbulent life. Hopefully, with this biography, something has.

Evelyn Dove

Augusta (Evelyn's mother)

Chapter 1: Evelyn's Family

In 1998, when Jeffrey Green published his book *Black Edwardians – Black People in Britain 1901–1914*, he told *The Independent* ('Historical Notes', 31 August): "The men, women and children of African birth or descent who lived in Britain at the beginning of this century—at the high noon of empire, when whites ruled the world—included every social group, but the black middle-class has been largely over-looked... Few have investigated the trail of evidence that is left by a property-owning, privately educated, servant-employing, professionally qualified person. Thus these black doctors, lawyers, businessmen, dentists, authors, local councillors and civil servants have disappeared from history."

Evelyn Dove's father, Frans Dove, falls into this category. He was a distinguished barrister who, throughout his life, was mostly based in Accra, the capital of the Gold Coast Colony, today's Ghana, but, as Jeffrey Green explains in *Black Edwardians*: "The African elite sought education in and professional qualifications from British institutions. Opportunities in Africa were extremely limited. Fourah Bay College in Sierra Leone attracted students from British West Africa... For those aspiring to become doctors and lawyers it was essential to have British qualifications. There had been Sierra Leonean medical students in Britain from the mid-nineteenth century." Green acknowledges that the composer Samuel Coleridge-Taylor (1875–1912), the London-born son of a Sierra Leonean doctor, was the most widely-known member of Edwardian Britain's black middle-class.

Frans Thomas's family also originated from Sierra Leone. He was born Francis Thomas Dove in 1869 at Freetown, Sierra Leone, the son of William Thomas Dove, a trader, and his wife, Mary Ann. Frans and his siblings were a family composed of lawyers, doctors and other highly educated professionals. When I interviewed Jeffrey Green in 1993, he explained that Evelyn's grandfather, William Dove, had made a fortune in trading from out of Freetown into the interior and thousands of miles along the coast beyond Nigeria: "His children were educated in England. Evelyn Dove's father was a barrister. Her uncle Frederick was a barrister. They had trading investments. They spent more of their time in Europe than they did in Africa. It was natural that the Doves married English women and it was natural also that their children were brought up in Britain. It may be a

Augusta (Evelyn's mother)

surprise to find out that there were many middle-class Africans who were more at home in England at the turn of this century and in the Edwardian era than they were in West Africa."

Frans was educated at the CMS Grammar School and later at Fourah Bay College in Sierra Leone. In 1886 he travelled to England to study law. He was admitted into the Honourable Society of Lincoln's Inn on 21 September 1888 and called to the Degree of Utter Barrister on 10 June 1891. He was enrolled as a Barrister of the Supreme Court on 6 July 1897 and that same year he began his practice in Accra. Meanwhile, in London in 1896, he married Evelyn's mother, Augusta Winchester.

Augusta was born on 3 March 1877 in Sandbanks, Hailsham in Sussex. Her father, John Winchester, was a gardener who had married her mother, Louisa Edmonds, in 1868. It is not known how Augusta and Frans met. Unlike in America, mixed marriages were not illegal in Britain and, as Jeffrey Green explains, middle-class African men who studied in Britain often married English women. Evelyn and her older brother, Frank (see Chapter 2) were educated privately, but Frans, based in West Africa, was a distant figure in their lives, though he provided for their education. Information about Evelyn's early years is limited, but she, her mother Augusta and brother Frank are listed among the passengers on the ship Zungeru which arrived at Liverpool on 23 September 1910 from Accra via Calabar, Nigeria (their port of departure). They were presumably returning from a visit to Evelyn's father Frans.

The 1911 Census confirms that Augusta, then age thirty-two, was living with nine-year-old Evelyn at 25A Barnard Road in the Wandsworth area of London. Beatrice, a sixteen-year-old servant, is also listed at the address. Evelyn's brother Frank was away at school. The First World War (1914–1918) probably enforced an even longer separation between Frans and his English wife and children, and it is understood that Frans and Augusta were divorced in 1920. Meanwhile, he fathered another daughter in Ghana, another "trailblazer", one who was to have an equally extraordinary life, but a character very different to Evelyn.

Journalist, political activist and creative writer Mabel Dove was born in Accra in 1905 to Eva Buckman, a Ghanaian businesswoman of Osu, Accra. At the age of six Mabel was sent to Freetown, Sierra Leone to be educated at a primary school run by her paternal aunt, Mrs Lydia Dove. She continued her education at the Annie Walsh Memorial School, also in Sierra Leone, before being sent to Britain to further her education. She was enrolled in the Anglican Convent in Bury St. Edmunds and St Michael's College. Against the wishes of her father, Mabel took a secretarial course. He promptly ordered her back to West Africa. However, Mabel was a determined young woman and, when the *West African Times* (renamed the *Times of West Africa* in 1933) was launched on 19 March 1931, she joined the staff. This was Ghana's first daily newspaper and it was edited by Dr. J. B. (Joseph Boakye) Danquah, a British-educated lawyer. In 1933 she married J. B. Danquah and they had a son, but the marriage was short-lived. Using the pseudonym 'Marjorie Mensah', Mabel was responsible for a column entitled "Ladies Corner" (renamed "Women's Corner" in 1933), from 1931 to 1935, when the newspaper folded. Her writing won her great popularity with readers and she encouraged her women readers to be inspired by the suffragette movement, to denounce imperialism, and to fight for women's rights. In their introduction to *Mabel Dove – Selected Writings of a Pioneer West African Feminist* (2004), Audrey Gadzekpo and Stephanie Newell describe Mabel as "a witty, educated and self-confident female voice" and said: "For many decades African women had contributed to the African-owned newspapers as letter-writers and occasional columnists, and since the inception of the West African press they had featured as the subjects of debates, but never before had the newspapers encountered such a dynamic and *daily* female presence."

Mabel continued working as a journalist and in 1951 she became the editor of the *Accra Evening News*, only the second woman to edit a newspaper in Ghana. After the war, Mabel became involved in politics and remained a loyal supporter of the Convention People's Party (CPP) and its leader, Kwame Nkrumah. Mabel was a prolific author over a period of four decades and her satire of George Bernard Shaw's *The Adventures of the Black Girl in Her Search for God* (1932), which she retitled *The Adventures of the Black Girl in Her Search for Mr Shaw*, was included in the British Library's 2015–2016 exhibition *West Africa: Word, Symbol, Song*. Mabel died in 1984.

Following their divorce in 1920, both Evelyn's parents remarried. Augusta married Frederic Montague Anson Ram, a widower of independent means, in Steyning, Sussex on 16 April 1929. They were both residing at 71 Walsingham Road, Hove. Frederic was the son of Reverend Robert Digby Ram, a Clerk in Holy Orders. He had been the Vicar of Hampton from 1882–1911 and died in 1925. Frederick Ram died in 1945 and not long afterwards Evelyn lost her beloved mother, Augusta, on 31 January 1947. Francis Thomas Dove, Evelyn's father, married Nellie Brown, a forty-one year old spinster, in London on 28 June 1929. He died in the Catholic Nursing Institute, 80 Lambeth Road, London on 22 August 1949 at the age of eighty, a few days after having undergone an operation. He was described on the death certificate as a Barrister-at-Law of Tudu House, Accra, Gold Coast, West Africa. In Accra, the

Evelyn sitting in the garden with her mother Augusta
and her step-father Frederic Montague Anson Ram

Daily Echo announced his passing in an issue published on 25 August:

There was an air of deep solemnity at the Chief Justice's Court yesterday morning when the Bench and Bar assembled to pay tribute to the memory of the late Mr. Francis Dove, Leader of the Gold Coast Bar, and President of the Bar Association. The assembly included not only the Practising Barristers, the District Magistrates, and the Judicial Staff of the Supreme Court, but also members of the deceased's family as well as notable personalities of the public. Mr Justice Mark Wilson, the Chief Justice, on behalf of himself and the Bench, addressed the Attorney-General and the members of the Bar in fitting terms. He said among other things that Mr Dove was the Father of the local Bar, and was called to the English Bar long years before most of the Judges were called.

The *Daily Echo* described Dove as "a grand old luminary of the legal profession" as well as a sportsman who was "the father here of the game of tennis." They added: "He was a man of high intelligence, and had left a gap which could be hardly filled." A few days later, the *Daily Echo* (31 August) announced that the body of 'Pa' Dove would arrive in Accra on 3 September. On 7 September they described his 'grand funeral' which took place at the Holy Trinity Cathedral in Accra: "On arrival the Church house had been filled to its utmost capacity with sympathisers both European and African including some high ranking government friends and ministers. In the Church the funeral service was conducted by His Lordship the Bishop of Accra." The *Daily Echo* report ended with a reference to Dove's "handsome" mansion at Tudu (a suburb of Accra) "which stands on two and a half acres of land with spacious tennis courts... The last time Mr Dove was heard of in public was the opening of the Colonial Month in London where he was presented to His Majesty King George VI. May his soul rest in peace!"

Francis Dove had been presented to King George VI and Queen Elizabeth at Church House in Westminster. Colonial Month took place from 21 June to 20 July 1949 with an exhibition at Oxford Street Hall about life in West Africa and other colonies throughout the British Empire. The opening ceremony and exhibition were filmed by the Colonial Film Unit and later shown across Africa. The commentator explained over a shot of West African men and Englishmen greeting each other outside the exhibition: "The Colonial Month gave British people and visitors from the colonies a great opportunity to meet and talk as these young men are doing here. It is small discussions like this that hold great hope for the future." The final shot shows the men waving and going their separate ways.

In 2003 I was contacted by Pauline Stewart who explained that Evelyn was a cousin of her father, Newton James Hodges:

His Aunt Augusta 'Gussie' was his mother Louise's sister. Aunt Gussie met Francis Dove who was, I believe, a wealthy lawyer from what was the Gold Coast. They had two children, Evelyn and Frank who, I think, was a boxer later on? You will appreciate that at that time a liaison between a white woman and a black man in a family was *not* well-received! My brother and I were not well-informed. It was a taboo subject. Evelyn Dove was never spoken of in my family home if my brother and I were in the room. We were then children and had no concept of racism in the 1930s. I do remember snatches of conversation from which I gathered that Evelyn was very glamorous. I also seem to recollect that my father's sister, Aunt Constance, said that Evelyn was in the London stage production of *South Pacific*. She went to see it and they met backstage. I do know that Aunt Gussie was known in the family as quite a gal! I just wish I had more information. One of my clearest memories is visiting Aunt Gussie with my parents in our car in the 1930s at her lovely house, The Old Manor House, Hurstpierpoint, Sussex. In 1936 my brother Peter and I stayed with Aunt Gussie when our parents went on a holiday abroad. I remember her husband Fredric Ram well. To a child (I was ten then) he was a very calm, gentle man. He had a live-in man servant, so perhaps he was not in good health. Aunt Gussie went to live nearer Brighton—possibly after Frederic's death. I remember hearing she was a very good swimmer when younger and that she swam the full distance between the two Brighton piers on more than one occasion. I am now seventy-seven, so of course my elders with any knowledge of Evelyn have long gone. I was sorry to find out what a sad ending to her life Evelyn endured. I do wish I had been more informed over the years and perhaps there would have been another person at her funeral. Thank you for sending me the lovely picture of Evelyn. I can see Aunt Gussie in her eyes.

Chapter 2: Frank Dove

Evelyn's older brother was born Francis Sydney Dove on 3 September 3 1897 at the City of London Lying-In Hospital for Married Ladies in City Road, Finsbury. Francis, popularly known as Frank, was educated at a boys' public school, Cranleigh, in the village of Cranleigh, Surrey. He was one of the school's first black pupils. Frank entered at the age of thirteen, in November 1910, unusually joining at half-term. He left in July 1915. His father is not listed as a contact, only his mother, Augusta, is named.

Cranleigh opened in 1865 as part of the boom in Victorian public school expansion. It aimed to provide its boys with a sound and plain education on the principles of the Church of England and on the public school system, for the sons of farmers and others engaged in commercial pursuits. It grew rapidly and by the 1880s had more than 300 pupils. By 1910 numbers had dropped to 150. Notable masters included Sir Michael Redgrave who taught at the school in the early 1930s before he became a famous actor. In *Secret Dreams – A Biography of Michael Redgrave* (2004), his biographer, Alan Strachan, described the Cranleigh of Redgrave's day as a school that "still preserved to a degree... the world of *Goodbye, Mr Chips*, with its arcane rituals, fagging and initiation rites, all the regulations of a well-oiled hierarchy."

Martin Williamson, Cranleigh School Archivist, told me: "Frank was a successful sportsman at Cranleigh and was in the 1st XI for football and cricket and was Hon Secretary of both sports. At that time Cranleigh did not play hockey or rugby so those were the two major sports. He was also one of the two gymnasts who represented Cranleigh at the Public Schools Gymnastic Competition at Aldershot—at the time a major event which Cranleigh had won five times, the most recent in 1913—where the school finished third overall. He was a school prefect and a bass in the choir. He was also a corporal in the Officers' Training Corp. The school magazine said he was 'a versatile member of the community both academically and athletically.'"

On leaving Cranleigh in July 1915, Frank was accepted to Merton College, Oxford to read law but he was called up in November 1916. It is a misconception that black British men were barred from joining the army. When Britain entered the First World War on 4 August 1914, some recruiting officers were unwelcoming, but many accepted black recruits and those black

Evelyn's brother Frank

Frank at Cranleigh School (1910)
Courtesy of Cranleigh School Archives

Britons who joined the army came from different social classes. Some came from the working class communities of the seaports, such as Harold Brown, who was born and raised in the dockland area of London's East End. He served as a private with the Royal West Surrey Regiment and his bravery in battle was recognised with two certificates of gallantry and the award of the Military Medal. Others, like Frank Dove, came from privileged families. Unlike the United States army, British regiments did not segregate black and white soldiers and Frank, who had successfully integrated into Cranleigh school life, was also integrated into army life.

According to his army service record, Frank's physical development was "excellent" and he confirmed that he was a British subject. The only clue to his African connections is the naming of his father, Frans Dove, as next-of-kin, and Accra, West Africa given as his father's address. Frank gave his home address as Brighton. On entering the army, Private Frank Dove joined the elite Royal Tank Corps where initially he served as a dispatch rider.

Frank received the Military Medal for his bravery at the battle of Cambrai in 1917. This was the first breach of the German lines in over three years. His army service record shows that Frank was "wounded on duty" in the field in December 1917 and granted leave. In June 1918, at the age of twenty, he proceeded to Britain for a Commission in the Cadet Unit of the Royal Air Force (RAF).

After being demobbed in 1920, Frank returned to Oxford to continue studying law. While there he boxed for the university and for Great Britain at the 1920 Summer Olympic Games in Antwerp in Belgium. At the Games, Frank was eliminated in the quarter-finals of the heavyweight class after losing his fight to the upcoming silver medallist, Soren Petersen. Frank continued to box while practising as a barrister and was still winning ABA divisional cruiserweight championships in 1945 by which time he was forty-seven. Frank qualified as a barrister and during the Second World War he served as an army officer.

Frank married Amelia Rawlinson (born 22 August 1895) in Brighton in 1919 and they had three children. He died on 10 February 1957 at the age of fifty-nine after being involved in a car accident in Wolverhampton. Amelia died in 1976 at the age of eighty.

In 2002 I located Olive, Frank and Amelia's eldest child. Olive explained that her younger sister Hazel had married and moved to America and her younger brother, Anthony 'Tony' Dove, had passed away from leukaemia in 1986 at the age of fifty-three. Regarding Evelyn, Olive said:

I was fascinated to read all the information you have gathered about my aunt, Evelyn Dove, and the rest of

Evelyn and Frank in the 1940s

the Dove family—much of which was unknown to me. When I was a child, it never occurred to me to ask questions. Also we were evacuated during the war from 1939 to 1944 and my father was away in the army so there was no sustained communication. After his father died in 1949, my father went to Africa to work as a lawyer and was killed in a car accident in Wolverhampton not long after he returned to this country in 1956. Of course I do have odd memories of Evelyn. She was very grand, like her mother Augusta, who was a Victorian lady; very austere. Evelyn had the most beautiful skin and my sister-in-law tells me that Evelyn only used margarine on her skin. I have no idea if it's true or not. I do remember some of the beautiful dresses she had made with wonderful boned bodices. I also remember going to see her when she was in *South Pacific*. Strangely enough I have no memory or idea why the family lost contact with her in the fifties and, unfortunately, there's no-one left to ask.

Chapter 3:
Royal Academy of Music/
Southern Syncopated Orchestra

Evelyn was born Evelyn Mary Dove at the Lying-In Hospital in Endell Street on 11 January 1902. Endell Street in London's West End runs from High Holborn in the north to Long Acre and Bow Street, Covent Garden, in the south. She was educated privately until, at the age of fifteen, she entered the Royal Academy of Music. According to surviving records in the Academy's archive, Evelyn joined during the autumn/winter term of 1917 and left in the summer of 1919. She studied singing, pianoforte and diction. At that time, the Academy awarded the Bronze medal, Silver medal and Certificate as levels of attainment; they were not related to any competition. Evelyn attained a Bronze medal for Singing in 1918 and a Silver medal for Singing in the following year. On 27 September 1919 Evelyn married Milton Alphonso Luke at Lambeth's Registry Office. Luke was a young, twenty-two-year old Trinidadian who had served in the British West Indies Regiment during the First World War. On their marriage certificate, Luke entered his profession as "student". It is not known what

happened to Alphonso Luke. Further research has not determined if Evelyn was widowed, or if the marriage ended in divorce.

With her graduation and marriage, 1919 was an important year for Evelyn, but it was also a landmark year for Britain's black community. It is generally accepted that the modern black community in Britain did not become established until *after* the arrival of the *Empire Windrush* in 1948. Most people believe that the settlement of people from Africa and the Caribbean didn't start until *after* the Second World War. However, this is not the case. In 1919 there was a significant number of African and Caribbean people living and working in Britain, and when the historian Jeffrey Green focussed his attention on London that year, he claimed in his article 'A Black Community? – London, 1919' in the journal *Immigrants and Minorities* (March 1986): "By 1919 London's blacks were numerous enough to publish a journal, to be victims of racial riots and to organise a group (the African Progress Union) which expressed opinions to the imperial

Young Evelyn

the direction of Cook, and with their leader and business manager George William Lattimore, the SSO journeyed to London for a series of concerts at the Philharmonic Hall. They remained here for several years, helping to introduce jazz music to Britain. The history of jazz is often focused on America, in particular New Orleans, but in 1919 the SSO took London and then the rest of Britain by storm. The SSO included thirty-five African American musicians. In *Under the Imperial Carpet – Essays in Black History 1780–1950* (1986) jazz historian Howard Rye says that the orchestra "brought with them in Sidney Bechet the first of the 'founding fathers' of New Orleans jazz to visit Europe; and they attracted the first critical notice of jazz which is known outside the pages of the black North American press. Their programmes were presented, however, in a context already familiar to European audiences: a mixture of minstrelsy, ragtime, spirituals, light-classical music and contemporary popular music." The SSO transformed the London club scene and popularised black music in Britain.

Evelyn's first encounter with the SSO was around the time she left the Royal Academy of Music. On 8 August 1919 Evelyn took part in a concert organised by the Coterie of Friends, a group of Caribbean (and one Ghanaian) students led by Edmund Thornton Jenkins. He was a respected member of London's black elite, having arrived in

government on matters relating to people of African descent. There was also an active group of students from Africa and the West Indies, an orchestra and choir from the United States, three medical practitioners of African descent, a sports club, several merchants and businessmen with a base in London, and enough soldiers and sailors to have their own meeting place in Drury Lane. There were also concerts organised by London's blacks and semi-formal gatherings where further contacts could be made. The fact that nearly every element had a link to another suggests that there was a black community in London in 1919."

The orchestra that Jeffrey Green referred to was the Southern Syncopated Orchestra (SSO), founded in New York by the composer and violinist Will Marion Cook. In 1919, under

Royal Academy of Music Silver Medal (1919) (front and back)

the metropolis in 1914 from America with the band from his father's orphanage to entertain at White City's Anglo-American Exposition. Jenkins remained in London and during the war he studied at the Royal Academy of Music. By 1919 he was teaching clarinet at the Academy. It was during that time he met the young Evelyn. Jenkins organised the concert in honour of an international group of representatives from the African-Caribbean colonies now visiting London. The delegates included men from Sierra Leone, the Gold Coast and Liberia. The event took place at the Albert Rooms, off Tottenham Court Road and Jenkins himself took part and played Weber's "Clarinet Concerto in F". Samuel Coleridge-Taylor's "Canoe Song" and Jenkins's lullaby "Baby Mine" were sung by Evelyn.

Evelyn joined the SSO in Glasgow in September 1921, using the name 'Norma Winchester', derived from her mother's birth name. By this time the SSO was under the direction of Egbert Thompson, who was born in Sierra Leone but had been raised in Jamaica. By 1921 the SSO included many members of African descent who, like Evelyn, were not American, as Howard Rye acknowledges in *Black Europe* (2013):

The original orchestra worked in London until the end of 1919, after which key personnel began to leave to seek more rewarding and stable employment than could be guaranteed by the management of an orchestra requiring such a large appearance fee to be economic. The dispersal of the African American personnel through first London night clubs and eventually throughout Europe played a major role in spreading African American performance practices, and especially rhythmic practices, across the continent. Meanwhile the orchestra's management filled the vacancies with members of the African diaspora from Europe, other parts of the Americas, and Africa, and when all else failed also employed local musicians who were not of African ancestry. As a result the orchestra became the ultimate jazz nursery with a central role in the history of jazz in Europe.

Rye notes that, by October 1921, when the orchestra was appearing in Glasgow, its members included several British people of African descent, including Evelyn, violinist James Boucher and singer Bert Marshall (real name Albert Essien).

Shortly after joining the SSO, Evelyn almost lost her life in a tragic incident involving the ship SS *Rowan*, which sank on its way from Scotland to Ireland. Howard Rye explains what happened in *Black Europe*:

On the evening of 8 October 1921, the orchestra embarked at Greenock aboard the Laird Line's *Rowan* for the journey to Ireland for an engagement in Dublin. Ironically, she was detained at Greenock for an hour and a half to suit the convenience of the orchestra. At 12.15 a.m. on the morning of 9 October, the vessel was off Coreswall Point, Wigtownshire, in thick fog when she was struck by an American steamer, the *West Camak* of Portland, Oregon, which was inbound to Glasgow from Seattle. This did little damage to either vessel but brought many passengers to the deck. Ten minutes later the *Rowan* was struck amidships by the liner *Clan Malcolm*, cutting her almost in two. She sank within three minutes.

In the best maritime tradition, Captain Donald Brown of the *Rowan* went down with his ship. Rescue work continued through the night with considerable success. Nine members of the orchestra were lost... The survivors, some of whom needed hospitalisation, regrouped in Glasgow. Many were destitute, having lost money and instruments and in some cases needing to borrow clothes. Two benefit concerts were held at which those fit to perform were joined by other performers appearing in Glasgow, including the African American act Scott and Whaley who were headlining at the Coliseum. Though still below strength for the first week, the orchestra resumed its projected Irish tour at the Lyric Theatre, Dublin, from 17 October 1921.

In 2013 the Nubian Jak Community Trust and Southwark Council honoured Frank Bates, lead singer with the SSO and a victim of the *Rowan* disaster, with a blue plaque on his former London home: 19 Hichisson Road, Peckham SE15. It is possible to view a silent Pathé newsreel film of Evelyn and other survivors of the SSO, in Dublin, originally issued on 24 October.

Following the *Rowan* disaster, Evelyn stayed with the SSO on their resumed Irish tour, and was with the orchestra in Vienna in August 1922, now calling herself "Evelyne Luke". A review in *The Aberdeen Daily Journal* (2 December 1921) attests to the bravery of the SSO who, in spite of the recent

October 1921 tragedy, and the loss of nine Orchestra members, enthused about their appearance at Aberdeen's Music Hall on 1 December: "A full house in the Music Hall, Aberdeen, greeted with rounds of applause last night's performances of the Southern Syncopated Orchestra... Perhaps the finest treat is the chorus. The voices of the singers blend in some wonderful sounds. At times they rise to a high pitch, and then lower to a great deep murmur, expressing varieties of emotion. Innumerable are the reasons why all music lovers should hear the programme of this group of players and singers. It is original and fresh. Like all music born of the need of song in a people, it appeals to the listener with that elemental truth of feeling in which race has no part and humanity is one."

As a classically trained singer, a contralto, Evelyn hoped to continue her career on the concert platform and possibly as an opera singer, but the worlds of variety, musical revue and cabaret were more welcoming.

On 9 October 1923 Evelyn took part in a concert in the Mortimer Hall, Mortimer Street, London. Evelyn sang "Nobody Knows" and also spirituals by H. T. Burleigh and items by Samuel Coleridge-Taylor, the acclaimed black British composer who had died in 1912. Samuel's daughter, Avril Coleridge-Taylor, also took part in the concert. Also British-born, Avril was a year younger than Evelyn. After her father's untimely death, Avril won a three-year scholarship

for Composition and Pianoforte to the Trinity College of Music in London. She also studied the violin, orchestration, composition and conducting. During her life (she died in 1998) Avril wrote more than ninety compositions and also worked as a conductor, rare for a woman of her time. Avril was one of the few women to break down barriers in the conservative, male-dominated world of classical music. On 21 May 1924 Evelyn and the African American baritone J. Francis Mores, accompanied by The Embassy Salon Orchestra, gave a Samuel Coleridge-Taylor song recital at Wigmore Hall. *The Era* (4 June 1924) noted that "Miss Evelyn Dove also sang. She looked particularly graceful in her crinoline of deep rose-coloured velvet, and made a highly decorative appearance on the platform. Her voice is charming, and so is her use of it."

That summer, Evelyn performed spirituals and plantation melodies with accompaniment by a harpist on a tour of British music halls. *The Era* (23 July 1924) was enthusiastic about Evelyn's appearance in a variety show at London's Alhambra in Leicester Square: "Other attractive items in the bill are Evelyn Dove, whose rare beauty enhances her interpretation of negro songs." She then appeared in August at London's Coliseum in Charing Cross, and in September in cabaret at Oddenino's Restaurant in Regent Street, London. *The Stage* (11 September 1924) published her photograph and noted: "Evelyn Dove,

the coloured singer of negro spirituals, is now proving her remarkable versatility by excellent performances of the lighter type of number. 'California Here I Come' and 'If You Do What You Do' are on her programme at Oddenino's Restaurant, and both numbers are brilliantly performed." Evelyn's next cabaret slot was the famous Café de Paris where she proved to be a sensation. *The Era* (1 October 1924) noted that "Evelyn Dove is scoring a sensational success at the Café de Paris, where she is featuring four great hits, 'California Here I Come', 'If You Do What You Do', 'I've Got a Cross-Eyed Pap' and 'Papa's Blues'. Miss Dove's charming personality and the 'big four' have taken the audience by storm."

It was around this time that Evelyn made her first recordings in London. With piano accompaniment she recorded four spirituals. Describing two of them in *Black Europe* (2013), Rainer E. Lotz, an authority on black music in Europe, notes: "'Couldn't Hear Nobody Pray' starts with some piano notes. Dove's Royal Academy of Music training and British diction are obvious. The song's simplicity is not spoiled by complex pianistics. She manages the swoops to high notes quite well. 'Ev'ry Time I Hear the Spirit' is a more joyous song, and is faster. The number and quality of performers of spirituals in early 1920s England was remarkable."

Evelyn returned to the Alhambra in Leicester Square in July 1925 for a variety show with Scott and Whaley and Jack

Hylton's band. *The Era* (18 July 1925) described her as "the beautiful Evelyn Dove, of the caressing voice and honey-coloured skin, sings negro spirituals and plantation lullabies charmingly." From at least May to July 1925, Evelyn was a member of the Southern Trio with two African Americans who had been associated with the SSO: John Payne and Clinton Rosemond. Payne had made London his home after the First World War and his apartment in Regent's Park Road became a base for many visiting African American artistes in the 1920s. These included Paul Robeson, Marian Anderson and Ethel Waters. Rosemond eventually returned to America where he acted in Hollywood films for many years. In addition to their stage appearances, the Southern Trio, with Evelyn, made three radio broadcasts for the BBC (see Chapter 10). When Evelyn left the Southern Trio to join the cast of the American revue *The Chocolate Kiddies* (see Chapter 4), she was replaced by another mixed-race Briton, Mabel Mercer. Unlike Evelyn, Mabel was illegitimate and the identity of her black father remained a mystery until she died. Born in Staffordshire, Mabel attended a Catholic convent school in Manchester before commencing a stage career. During the First World War she worked in music halls, and joined the casts of several Will Garland shows (see Chapter 5) including *Coloured Society* (1916–17). After basing herself in Paris for several years, Mabel returned to Britain to

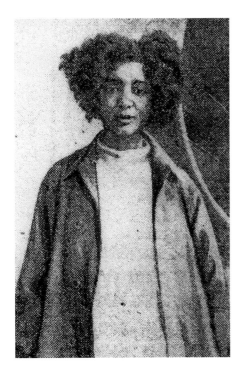

Unidentified newspaper cutting of Evelyn after she survived the SS *Rowan* disaster (1921)

replace Evelyn in the Southern Trio in mid-1925 before joining the casts of two successful West End shows: *Blackbirds* (1926) starring Florence Mills and *Show Boat* (1928) starring Paul Robeson. Returning to Paris, Mabel began her long and successful career as a cabaret singer. She was perhaps the greatest cabaret artiste of her generation and, after relocating to New York in 1938, she influenced some of the great American singers of the twentieth century. Among them were Billie Holiday, Barbra Streisand and Frank Sinatra who once told a journalist "Mabel Mercer taught me everything I know about a lyric." In 1983 Mabel was awarded America's Presidential Medal of Freedom.

To Mother,
from
Evie.

FOTO
Ahlberg's Paris

Chapter 4: *The Chocolate Kiddies*

In July 1993 I visited the ninety-one-year old jazz singer Adelaide Hall at her West Kensington home. It was the last time I saw Adelaide in person. We had been friends for about ten years and, though we spoke on the phone after the July visit, she passed away later that year on 7 November. During this final visit, I asked Adelaide if she remembered Evelyn Dove with whom she was featured in a 1925 stage revue called *The Chocolate Kiddies*. She said:

That was way back. Evelyn was an English girl and came from England to replace Lottie Gee in *Chocolate Kiddies*. She was doing something important in London, a cabaret or something. I had a star part. Evelyn was in the cast with us in Europe. She was a really lovely girl and very pretty. She sang "Joshua Fit the Battle of Jericho". We travelled to Germany and other places. I remember Evelyn sang well and looked very good.

The Chocolate Kiddies was a revue put together in New York to give European audiences a taste of African American entertainment. By 1925 New York had established itself as the 'Black Capital of the World' and the Harlem Renaissance was in full swing. America witnessed a large-scale explosion of creative energy and artistic expression from a range of talented African American entertainers, jazz musicians, artists and intellectuals, and the event most frequently acknowledged as marking the beginning of this period was the Broadway musical *Shuffle Along*, which opened in 1921 and ran for 504 performances, unprecedented for an all-black cast show. Adelaide Hall was one of its stars and Josephine Baker made her stage debut in the chorus. In 1940 the writer Langston Hughes explained in *The Big Sea*: "The 1920s were the years of Manhattan's black Renaissance [and] it was the musical revue, *Shuffle Along*, that gave a scintillating send off to that Negro vogue in Manhattan, which reached its peak just before the [Wall Street] crash of 1929... It gave just the proper push—a pre-Charleston kick—to that Negro vogue of the 20s that spread to books, African sculpture, music and dancing." In the next four years another ten black Broadway shows opened in New York, but none of them were staged outside the United States.

In New York, in addition to stage musicals and revues, nightclubs like the Cotton Club, Small's Paradise and Connie's Inn showcased talented

African Americans and the artistes enjoyed unprecedented success and popularity in white and urban black America. But there was an unpleasant side to this, as the singer Lena Horne (whose career was launched at the Cotton Club in 1933), later explained in her autobiography *Lena* (1965):

Nostalgia has not played anyone false about the Cotton Club shows. They were wonderful. But for the employees, it was an exploitative system... The club got great talent very cheap, because there were so few places for great Negro performers to work... As for the 'exotic', wonderful, rhythmic, happy-go-lucky quality of our lives, that was a real joke. Especially for my family. We lived in a typical, roach-infested tenement.

Before *The Chocolate Kiddies*, European audiences hadn't seen many black jazz orchestras or entertainers, so this was a breakthrough. Josephine Baker did not arrive in Paris and become an international star with *La Revue Nègre* until October 1925. Sam Wooding's orchestra was chosen to play with the *Kiddies* revue, and a young Duke Ellington and Jo Trent wrote a few of the songs that were featured. Some of the musicians and acts were found at New York's Club Alabam on West 44th Street, including Wooding and Adelaide Hall. They found the singer Lottie Gee in the cast of Noble Sissle and Eubie Blake's Broadway show *The Chocolate*

Dandies. With a cast that included more than thirty chorus girls, dancers and comedians, *Chocolate Kiddies* set sail from New York to Germany in May 1925. Adelaide Hall, one of the stars of the revue, remembered the excitement of travelling abroad for the first time, and how the producers of *Chocolate Kiddies* hired top black acts from various stage productions and nightclubs to take part:

It was a beautiful show and we had over thirty performers in the cast. We had tap dancers and singers. Sam Wooding led the orchestra and the music was jazz oriented. It was marvellous and it gave Europeans their first opportunity to see black singers and dancers. That's why the revue was such a success, because people in Europe hadn't seen anything like it. *The Chocolate Kiddies* opened in Germany and then we went to Sweden, Denmark, Eastern Europe, Spain, France, Switzerland and Russia, where the company performed for Stalin. But I only went as far as Copenhagen. My husband, Bert, wanted me to come home.

The *Chocolate Kiddies* company sailed for Europe on 6 May 1925 on board S.S. *Arabic* of the American White Star Line. They arrived in Hamburg on 17 May and in Berlin on 18 May. They had one week before opening night and an opportunity to explore the famous capital of Germany. However, Adelaide Hall recalled that, on the streets and in shops and cafes,

Evelyn on her travels in the 1920s

Evelyn on her travels in the 1920s

"Many Berliners were hostile towards us because they thought we were French Colonial Africans, whom they hated. It had to be made clear to Berliners that we were from America." On opening night at the Admiral's Palace on 25 May, the reception was encouraging. In *Jazz from the Beginning* (1988), Garvin Bushell, one of Sam Wooding's celebrated musicians, recalled: "The audience whistled and hollered 'Bravo'. At first we thought they were screaming at us, 'Beasts, beasts!' Then we learned they were calling out 'Bis! Bis!' for encores. Most of the numbers had to take several encores."

Chocolate Kiddies conformed to a romanticised reflection of African American life by staging the songs and dances on the cotton fields of a southern plantation, a jungle and a Harlem cabaret. Garvin Bushell said the show was built around Rufus Greenlee and Thaddeus Drayton, a big time vaudeville act in the United States. They had worked in Europe before the First World War and, Bushell recalled, "They'd come out dancing and talk in all these different languages. They'd start with Hungarian, then they'd speak Russian, then French, Yiddish, English, and finally wind up in German." Bushell also remembered The Three Eddies (Shaky Beasley, Tiny Ray and 'Chick' Horsey) who wore bowler hats, round-rimmed spectacles, white gloves and spats, and worked in blackface: "They were very fast and funny, with great singing and dancing. Back at the Club Alabam they used to break up the show nightly." Before the end of the decade, 'Chick' Horsey had left The Three Eddies to work with Evelyn as a double-act.

Towards the end of 1924 Evelyn had been taken under contract by Dr Sirota, manager of London's Gaiety Theatre. Sirota was the road manager of the *Chocolate Kiddies* revue for their European tour. Lottie Gee was one of the star attractions of the revue, but when she unexpectedly decided to return home at the end of the Berlin engagement, a replacement had to be found at short notice. Dr Sirota contacted Evelyn and she readily agreed to be added to the cast as the only non-American, when the revue moved from Berlin to Hamburg, where they opened at the Thalia Theatre on 22 July. Evelyn is named as a featured soloist in the Hamburg programme. A comparison of Lottie's Berlin and Evelyn's Hamburg programmes reveals that Lottie's songs had been given to Evelyn to perform. It proved to be a wonderful showcase for Evelyn.

Chocolate Kiddies opened on a southern plantation with Arthur 'Strut' Payne singing "Old Black Joe". This was followed by Evelyn singing "Joshua Fit the Battle of Jericho", a song believed to have been composed by slaves, and Stephen Foster's slave's lament, "Swanee River", also known as "Old Folks at Home". In the final part of the revue, the "Harlem Cabaret segment", the first scene had Adelaide Hall and the Chocolate Kiddies on stage singing and dancing to Duke Ellington's "Deacon Jazz". This was followed by Evelyn singing "The Red Rose". The entire company returned to the stage for a furious finale.

When Evelyn arrived in Kobenhavn [Copenhagen, Denmark] with the *Chocolate Kiddies*, she was interviewed for the weekly Danish magazine *Vore Damer*. In the published interview she claims to have been born in Sierra Leone,

West Africa and adopted at the age of three months by an English married couple who were "passing through"! Here is a translation:

HOTEL HAFNIA, room no. 35, – "Come in" – said by a mezzo soprano. A slightly coloured lady of the world, Miss Evelyn Dove asks us to take a seat and in a few sentences tells us the story of her life. "I was born in Sierra Leone, West Africa and 3 months old I parted from my parents and was adopted by an English married couple who passed through the town at that time. London then became my place of residence and here I went to school. When I was 18 I went on the stage and so far I have been very lucky. My present manager, Dr Sirota, spotted me a few years back at The Gaiety Theatre in London. It was he who told me on the phone that in Hamburg I could take over the part I now play with the *Chocolate Kiddies*. Even though I have only been in Copenhagen for a week I can say that I feel more at home here than in England—the English are a little too dry and phlegmatic for me. On this tour, which is going to last for 9 months more, I'll probably have an eventful time and meet with a lot of interesting people, but do please remember me to all Copenhageners and tell them I would have loved to stay here forever."

Though the *Chocolate Kiddies* revue continued touring Europe until the end of 1925, and into 1926, at the end of an engagement in Kobenhavn in September 1925 Evelyn left the cast and returned to London. In *Black Music in the Harlem Renaissance – A Collection of Essays*, edited by Samuel A. Floyd Jr (1995), Jeffrey Green suggests in his essay 'The Negro Renaissance in England' that another "Harlem Renaissance" took place in Britain: "The occurrence of a Harlem Renaissance in England seems unlikely, if not absurd, but New York did not have sole possession of the ideals that led to the black artistic outflow of the Renaissance." One the most outstanding stage personalities who made a successful crossover from New York to London was the singer and dancer Florence Mills (1895–1927). In 1923 the great British theatrical impresario C. B. Cochran starred her in his West End revue *Dover Street to Dixie*. Three years later Cochran brought her back to London for one her greatest stage successes, *Blackbirds*. In 1994 when I interviewed Elisabeth Welch about Florence, she remembered her as "sweet and loved by everybody. She was treated as a great star and with great respect. People adored her." After her return to London in September 1925, Evelyn took advantage of the success and popularity of Florence Mills, and pursued her career with great success in Britain, and later Europe.

Chapter 5: Will Garland's *Brownbirds*

After leaving the cast of *Chocolate Kiddies*, Evelyn made regular appearances in cabaret at The Queen's in Leicester Square. An ambitious Evelyn then put together a song and dance troupe of her own: Evelyn Dove and Her Plantation Creoles. Advertised as "the only singing and dancing act of its kind in Europe", one of their many engagements included a successful appearance at the Winter Garden, Berlin in October 1926. After Berlin, the troupe appeared in the Netherlands and then in Paris. From January until the end of March 1927 the troupe was at the Hotel Negresco in Nice,

sharing the bill with the Sam Wooding Orchestra in *Revue Nègre*. In May 1927 Evelyn was back in Berlin before she returned to Britain and joined the cast of Will Garland's revue *Brownbirds*.

In July 1929 the Jamaican trumpeter Leslie Thompson arrived in Britain and discovered that Archer Street and Charing Cross Road, in the heart of London's West End, were the places for musicians to look for work in the entertainment business. Thompson had heard about a show that was touring called *Brownbirds* and that its producer, the African American showman, Will Garland, was providing employment for black artists and musicians. Thompson met with Garland who invited him to join the show's orchestra. "So I did," Thompson told Jeffrey Green in *Swing from a Small Island* (2009), "for about four weeks, and we toured to Brighton, and Bristol, and a couple of other places."

Thompson remembered Garland as a very experienced showman. In addition to being in

Winter Garden, Berlin (1926)

Evelyn and her Plantation Creoles (1926)

charge of *Brownbirds*, "he sang, and did comedy routines."

In fact, Garland had arrived in Britain in the Edwardian era and had quickly established himself with all-black cast shows with titles like *Coloured Society*, *All-Black*, *Down South* and *Coloured Lights*. Garland's shows were popular with British audiences, especially during the First World War, and they were very much in keeping with the American format of such shows, with scenes set on plantations, African villages and a nightclub. In 1917 *The Stage* newspaper reviewed *Coloured Society*:

The scenes, which number seven, include a Zulu village, Uncle Ham's log cabin and a ballroom; and the company includes some clever dancers and agreeable vocalists. A feature is made of the rendering of the choruses of some well-known melodies, which are much enjoyed by those in front. (*The Stage*, 20 September 1917)

In addition to providing work for visiting or ex-patriate African Americans, Garland's shows also gave opportunities to black Britons from all walks of life, but mostly the black communities of the seaports of London's East End, Cardiff and Liverpool. These included comedians, singers and chorus girls. In 1929 his *Brownbirds* toured Britain with Evelyn as the lead female singer. Leslie Thompson remembered her and the format of the show which, apart from the title, Garland had hardly changed since the First World War:

There was one scene, with Evelyn Dove with a Mammy's head scarf, and the chorus girls gathered round her. She sang all those Mammy songs—"Mighty Lak a Rose", "Swing Low Sweet Chariot", "I Got a Robe"—that sort of thing. She had a very fine voice. She had been in Paris and all over Europe, as had Will Garland. One of the male dancers was Stanley Coleman, a British lad, a coloured lad. He was a quiet chap, a little effeminate. There was a troupe of a dozen coloured girls. One was Lily Jemmott. She was from Cardiff, and she played the piano, and danced. Years later she married Dr Dele Alakija. It was a good road show, and we got the audiences.

In his book *Black People – Entertainers of African Descent in Europe, and Germany* (1997), Rainer E. Lotz describes Will Garland as a theatrical entrepreneur who was "able to keep going over a period of several decades... Garland gave employment to both white and black men and women, and all of them experienced the perils of show business. Being black and an American made him experience additional hazards of a social and professional nature... his career reflects a consistent level of attainment within his chosen profession." William Garland died in London on 25 November 1938 at the age of sixty-two.

Evelyn and her partner
'Chick' Horsey, touring
in Italy in the 30s

Chapter 6: Italy and France

The main source of information for Evelyn Dove's stage tours of Italy is Adriano Mazzoletti's *Il Jazz in Italia*, originally published in Italy in 2004. With a translation by the British jazz historian Howard Rye, it is possible to chronicle Evelyn's Italian diary. Reviews are attributed to *Il Mattino*, an Italian daily newspaper, published in Naples.

From 17 to 27 January 1930 Evelyn and her ensemble were featured at the Teatro Maffei, Turin, accompanied by the orchestra of the African American jazz violinist Leon Abbey. In the 1920s Abbey's band was considered one of the best in jazz. Throughout the 1920s and 1930s Abbey took his band on extended tours of South America, Europe and India. The *Mattino* gave the show a title: *Biano e Nero e Viceversa* (*Black & White & Vice-Versa*) and described it as "a grand spectacle in three parts and maybe this, of its type, is the richest spectacle which has been offered to the Turin public." At the Teatro Maffei, the revue ensemble included dancer Layburn 'Chick' Horsey, who had also been with Evelyn in the *Chocolate Kiddies* revue.

Evelyn on stage in Italy (1930s)

On 5 and 6 October 1930 Evelyn and the Abbey orchestra appeared at the Trocadero, Napoli and, on 11 and 12 October, 'Evelyn Dove and Leon Abbey with the Dixie Steppers' performed at the Sala Umberto in Rome.

The *Mattino* was enthusiastic:

Yesterday evening at the Sala Umberto theatre gave the impression of a great occasion, without an empty seat. All fashionable Rome convened on this date to assist at the debut of the creole Evelyn Dove, who in combination with the famous Negro jazz of Leon Abbey earned warm and sincere applause. Negro song and dance followed one another, and Leon Abbey's jazz was especially applauded for his unmatchable creativity.

From early 1931 Evelyn, with 'Chick' Horsey as her partner, toured throughout Italy with her own revue ensemble. After an evening party in her honour at the Teatro Nuovo in Naples on 4 January, Evelyn appeared at the same theatre from 15 to 21 January. The tour ended at the Verdi in Firenze from 17 to 21 November. The *Mattino* reported: "Acclaimed success yesterday evening went to the new grand programme of variety built around Evelyn Dove, the same creole returning to more significant success. Miss Dove essays a beautiful repertoire of exotic songs linked to her dancing, and the contributions of the Negroes 'Chick Horsey' and Al Wilkins." The day after, the *Mattino*

again reported, "Large farewell party in honour of Evelyn Dove and her Negro troupe". Unfortunately, the name of the orchestra which accompanied this show is not cited by the newspapers of the time, which focused on presenting the three stars, Dove, Horsey, and Wilkins.

During the summer of 1932 the ensemble was in Italy with 'Chick' Horsey as Evelyn's dance partner; the programme was accompanied by a band led by African American trombonist Frank Withers. In 1934 Evelyn toured Italy with the dancer and choreographer Louis Douglas, accompanied by the American Boys Jazz Band of Italian pianist and violinist Romero Alvera. In December 1935, Evelyn Dove sailed from Napoli to New York.

As early as 1935 there was evidence of growing anti-Jewish as well as anti-black American bias in the worlds of entertainment in Austria, Germany, and Italy. Marian Anderson was among the African American artists denied permission to perform in Germany and Austria—including the cancellation of a scheduled recital at the Salzburg festival in Vienna on 18 August 1935—on the grounds of being non-Aryan. In Mussolini's Italy, anti-black American sentiment became so strong that the American consul in Rome advised black American entertainers not to accept contracts to appear in Italy, as contracts were likely not to be honoured. Lew Lake's musical revue *Blackberries*, which was rehearsing at Lake Como for an

Evelyn performing in Italy (1930s)

opening in Rome, received an official notice banning the show. The theatre company was forced to return to London. In Germany, though Adolf Hitler spoke favourably of the singer Paul Robeson in 1932, he was also reported saying: "Negroes must be definitely third-class people… a hopeless lot. I don't hate them. I pity the poor devils."

The Casino de Paris was one of the most popular music halls of Paris, with a history dating back to the 18th century. For decades all the great French stars played in shows at the Casino de Paris including Mistinguett, Maurice Chevalier and Josephine Baker. From humble beginnings in the slums of St Louis to international stardom, Josephine Baker made her name in Paris in 1925 when she journeyed there from America

Replacing Josephine Baker
at the Casino de Paris, 1930s

Evelyn performing
in Italy (1930s)

with *La Revue Nègre* which opened at the Theatre des Champs Elysées. Hungry for success, she made her entrance almost entirely nude (except for a pink flamingo feather tucked between her thighs) and performed the erotic "Dance of the Savages". Playing on European audience's racist view of black women as exotic primitives, Josephine was a sensation and news of her appearance swept throughout Europe. Overnight the nineteen-year-old runaway from St Louis became the toast of Paris. The French adored her, couldn't get enough of her and she adopted France as her home. Under the guidance of her lover, Pepito Abatino, Josephine was transformed into a beautiful, glamorous, bejewelled star of the great Parisian music halls, including the Folies Bergère and the Casino de Paris. Flaunting convention, Josephine symbolised a new kind of freedom for women.

It is highly likely that Evelyn would have seen Josephine at this time. Evelyn had also arrived in Europe in 1925, and continued working there for a number of years. Another mixed-race Londoner, Josie Woods, also worked in Paris in the late 1920s. Josie was born in Canning Town in London's East End to a black (Dominican) dock worker and his wife, whom Josie later described as "a gypsy girl... or so she told us!" In Britain in the 1920s there were few job openings for a working-class black girl in the days when they left school at fourteen. Indeed, Josie chose the stage because she said it was very hard in those days for black people

to get a job. In 1927 the fifteen-year-old successfully auditioned for Belle Davis, a veteran black entertainer (see Chapter 9) who had been popular in Edwardian music halls. Josie's mother said to Miss Davis, "Why can't you take her? She can't keep still!" So Josie joined Miss Davis's dance troupe, the Magnolia Blossoms. Josie later described herself as "something the cat dragged in, this little girl from the East End, a scruffy little thing." But she was determined to achieve success as a dancer and happily travelled with Miss Davis and the Magnolia Blossoms to Paris and the Continent where they remained for two years. In Paris Josie saw her namesake, Josephine Baker, on

she sang spirituals. I thought she was very straight-laced, a true prim and proper middle-class English girl. When word got back to her family that she had appeared on stage, semi-naked, they were horrified and I think her father disowned her.

Josie continued her stage career in Britain into the 1950s and died in 2008 at the age of ninety-six. The actress Cleo Sylvestre remembers the fun she had as a child in the 1950s, visiting Josie in Brixton with her mother who had once danced with her: "When my mother took me to see Josie there was lots of laughter. She was a very happy-go-lucky lady. Never down. Always very positive. Sometimes Josie would jump up and do a little dance for me."

stage. On returning to London, she saw Evelyn Dove on stage in Will Garland's revue *Brownbirds*.

When I interviewed Josie in 1997, she recalled:

It would have been in the 1930s that Evelyn went to France and replaced Josephine Baker as the star attraction in a revue at the Casino de Paris. She looks just like Josephine Baker in the photo, doesn't she? And she was sometimes referred to as Britain's Josephine Baker. But when she did this, she scandalised her family. Her father was a respectable West African lawyer and her mother was, by all accounts, a "grand" Englishwoman. Evelyn had had a private education and had studied at the Royal Academy of Music. Before she went to Paris, I remember seeing her on stage in *Brownbirds* when

Chapter 7: Cabaret Queen in New York

In his biography of Bessie Smith, *Bessie – Empress of the Blues* (1972), the blues and jazz historian Chris Albertson described New York's Harlem nightlife in the 1920s and 1930s and the three top nightclubs that attracted the crowds:

Night after night the bejewelled and befurred flocked to black Harlem from their homes on Park Avenue or Riverside Drive to hear the great black entertainers at Small's Paradise, Connie's Inn, or the Cotton Club. There they were assured an elaborate show in an atmosphere that seemed congenial, even though some of these clubs appeared to have a whites-only policy. Actually, few black people could afford the high prices... Shedding their inhibitions along with their furs—feeling adventurous among the natives—whites would round off an evening in Harlem.

Evelyn entered this world towards the end of 1935 when she was offered a cabaret engagement at Connie's Inn. Until then, no black British star had ever been offered such an opportunity in America. Evelyn was the first. Evelyn arrived in New York from Naples on 20 November 1935 on the ship *Rex*. On the passenger register she is listed Eveline (sic) Augusta Dove, age 33, artiste, English. The African American press noted her arrival and her apparent rivalry with Josephine Baker. Said *The Afro American* (18 January 1936):

The arrival of Miss Dove has sharpened interest both in Harlem and Broadway because of the widely heralded rivalry between her and the Countess Josephine. Harlem is also wondering just how this continental star will be received by Broadway because she had none of the mannerisms or *hotcha* tactics usually expected of artists of colour. She is refreshingly different from anything Dixie or Harlem has had to offer. She speaks with a foreign accent which is as much Italian as it is French. Only rarely does she revert to English and then one detects the added H's that distinguish enunciation of the Londoner.

However, Evelyn may not have been aware that she was arriving in New York at a time when Josephine was also about to return to New York, after a long absence, for an appearance in a lavish Broadway revue. And another rivalry was being talked about, that of Josephine and the popular African American star Ethel Waters who had just opened in her revue on Broadway to great acclaim.

On her arrival in New York Evelyn was invited to sit for the portrait photographer Carl Van Vechten, the white patron of the Harlem Renaissance. Throughout the 1930s he photographed numerous show business celebrities. Among the famous black stars photographed by Van Vechten were Marian Anderson, Josephine Baker, Billie Holiday, Mabel Mercer, Paul Robeson, Bessie Smith, Ethel Waters and Elisabeth Welch. Van Vechten photographed Evelyn at his New York studio on 27 December 1935. These can be viewed online in the Carl Van Vechten's Portraits collection in the Beinecke Rare Book and Manuscript Library.

Evelyn's engagement at Connie's Inn was an important one. At the height of the Harlem Renaissance, Connie's Inn—with Small's Paradise and the Cotton Club—were the three most publicised clubs frequented by white high society and famous celebrities. Connie's Inn, situated at 2221 Seventh Avenue, occupied a large basement in a building at the corner of 131st Street and Seventh Avenue. Says Arnold Shaw in *The Jazz Age – Popular Music in the 1920s* (1987):

When it opened in 1921, it called itself Shuffle Inn as a tribute to the Noble Sissle and Eubie Blake Broadway hit show, *Shuffle Along*. After a short time the place was bought by George and Connie Immerman, who were in the delicatessen business and who employed Fats Waller as their delivery boy. The Immermans altered the entrance from the 131st Street side to Seventh Avenue where it opened in June 1923. Like its luxurious competitors, Connie's featured elaborate floor shows.

The popularity of Connie's Inn peaked in 1929 when Louis Armstrong headlined its most successful floor show, *Hot Chocolates*, written by Fats Waller and Andy Razaf. It featured such song hits as "Ain't Misbehavin'". It is said that this floor show, which moved to the Broadway stage, was the beginning of Louis Armstrong's greatest fame. Of the "Big Three" nightclubs popular with white patrons, the Cotton Club was considered the most opulent. It was most famous for presenting first rate floor shows, known as the Cotton Club Parades that attracted and starred a succession of legendary African American entertainers like Cab Calloway, Ethel Waters and Adelaide Hall. The floor shows were so good they rivalled Broadway musicals.

It was Ethel Waters who made a successful transition from the Cotton Club to "white" Broadway revues. In 1933, after launching the famous torch song "Stormy Weather" at the Club, Ethel joined the white cast of the Broadway revue *As Thousands Cheer*. She was one of the few black stars to have achieved this. Her appearance was a triumph, and her songs, written by America's foremost composer Irving Berlin, included "Heat Wave" and "Supper Time". Two years

later Ethel was offered a second chance to co-star in a "white" Broadway revue, *At Home Abroad*. It opened at the Winter Garden Theatre on 19 September 1935. This proved to be another personal triumph for her, elevating her to even more national fame and popularity, unprecedented in America for a black female star.

Ethel's "rivalry" with the legendary Josephine Baker reached a peak at this time when Josephine, an expatriate who had made her home in France ten years earlier, decided to return to America and follow Ethel into the Winter Garden Theatre with a lavish revue called *Ziegfeld Follies of 1936*. Josephine's show opened on 30 January 1936. Therefore two of America's most famous black female stars were integrated into "white" Broadway shows in quick succession. Comparisons were inevitable, as were rumours of rivalry. For Josephine, the comparison between herself and Ethel, whom she had once understudied, was a sore subject. And when Ethel tried to visit Josephine to wish her luck with the *Follies*, Josephine snubbed her. Josephine allegedly described Ethel's songs as "colored mammy, back to Alabammy" material, songs Josephine avoided singing in France. However, Irving Berlin's "Supper Time", about lynching in the south, which Ethel had sung in *As Thousands Cheer*, could hardly be described in that way. It is more likely that Ethel's clever and funny parody of Josephine

(Irving Berlin's "Harlem on My Mind") in the same revue is what upset the expatriate. Ethel had the last laugh. She was riding high after the success of *At Home Abroad*, while Josephine received a critical drubbing for the *Follies* and humiliations away from the theatre.

At the end of October 1935, Josephine sailed from France to New York on the *Normandie*, but on her arrival she was turned away from the hotel where she had reservations with her husband, 'Pepito' Abatino. The hotel did not want to risk offending their white Southern guests by allowing a black woman to stay on their premises. Josephine discovered that nothing had changed in America since her 1925 departure for Paris. When *Follies* opened, critics complained about the smallness of her voice, not appreciating that the Winter Garden Theatre was twice the size of the Folies Bergère in Paris which often showcased Josephine. At the opening night party, hosted by the lyricist Lorenz Hart, Josephine was subjected to a put down by a member of her own race when, overheard speaking in fluent French to Hart and his famous guests, Hart's black maid allegedly pulled Josephine aside and confronted her: "Girl, why don't you talk the way yo' mouth was born?"

The African American entertainer Maude Russell was approached and asked if she would be interested in replacing Josephine in *Follies*, as she later explained to Josephine's adopted son Jean-Claude Baker in his biography *Josephine* (1993):

They wanted a replacement for Josephine because she wasn't going over. They said she was acting up and they were fixing to get rid of her. At that time, nobody wanted to see a coloured girl being twirled around with four white boys and dressed up like a queen. All those people were saying, "She's black, trying to be white, why don't she go on and be her original self when she was stickin' her fanny out and looking ugly?"

Josephine eventually left the *Follies* and returned to France. Rumours of starring roles in Hollywood movies remained just rumours. America was not ready to embrace a beautiful, glamorous black female star. This would begin to change in the following decade, the 1940s, when the singer Lena Horne took Hollywood by storm, and Katherine Dunham graced the Broadway stage with her wonderful dance troupe.

In his biography of Ethel Waters, *Heat Wave – The Life and Career of Ethel Waters* (2011), Donald Bogle says: "Baker and Waters must have realised they had a price to pay by breaking down Broadway barriers. Would they ever be treated as equals? For the Negro press, Baker was the slim princess, Ethel was the duchess. No one liked seeing the way Black royalty was being treated."

On reflection, considering how America treated Ethel and Josephine, Evelyn didn't stand a chance of finding fame in America, but at least she tried. She was disadvantaged even before she

opened at Connie's Inn. When Evelyn arrived in New York, the Connie's Inn floor show *Stars Over Broadway* was a big success and a hard act to follow. Earlier in 1935, Joe Glaser had taken over the management of an up-and-coming young jazz singer called Billie Holiday. The first booking he got for Billie was the *Stars Over Broadway* revue. By this time, like the Cotton Club, Connie's Inn had moved downtown, to 48th Street between Broadway and Seventh Avenue. *Stars Over Broadway* opened at Connie's Inn on 29 October 1935 and it also starred the jazz legend Louis Armstrong and the dancer Earl 'Snakehips' Tucker. The revue was a success, but in January 1936 Billie became ill and had to leave the show. She was replaced by Bessie Smith, the legendary singer known as the "Empress of the Blues". So, in January 1936, Evelyn had the distinction—or disadvantage— of following Billie Holiday *and* Bessie Smith, two giants of American blues and jazz, into Connie's Inn.

Needless to say, Ralph Matthews, a reporter, made a big deal of Evelyn's New York debut in *The Afro American* (18 January 1936), hoping to attract audiences to her show. Headlined "Rival of Jo Baker to Make Broadway Bow— Evelyn Dove Precedes the Countess to gay White Way", here is a transcript of the article:

A sudden change in the theatrical set up in New York's Broadway will bring Evelyn

Macari
Napoli - Roma

Dove, the London-born bronze sensation, into the main stem fully two weeks ahead of her Continental rival, Mlle. Josephine Baker, who was imported from Paris as one of the stars of *Ziegfeld Follies*. Miss Dove, a tall, sylphlike songbird, who is the daughter of a prominent London barrister holding a royal post in British West Africa, will open at Connie's Inn Friday night, in a specially constructed revue on which Ted Blackman, the Connie's Inn producer, is working feverishly. Miss Dove arrived in America three weeks ago but was not scheduled to open until the present production featuring Louis Armstrong and an array of stars completed its run. The whole aspect changed late last week when the Connie management learned through the grapevine telegraph that three of their rival clubs had been secretly rehearsing new shows and planned to spring them this week. Such a strategic move would have left the club featuring the greatest stars high and dry. So Miss Dove's opening was speeded up to meet the competition. The arrival of Miss Dove has sharpened interest both in Harlem and Broadway because of the widely heralded rivalry between her and the Countess Josephine. Harlem is also wondering just how this continental star will be received by Broadway because she had none of the mannerisms or *hotcha* tactics usually expected of artists of color. She is refreshingly different from anything Dixie or Harlem has had to offer. She speaks with a foreign accent which is as much Italian as it is French. Only rarely does she revert to English and then one

detects the added H's that distinguish enunciation of the Londoner. Miss Dove is a prize-winning graduate of the Royal Academy of Music in London and started her career as a concert artist under the direction of George W. Lattimore, the European agent, who has introduced many stars to Europe. As soon as he is assured of Miss Dove's success here he will hasten back to the continent where he will attend the Monte Carlo debut of Caterina Jarbaro, whose tour he is also managing. He is a native Harlemite, and was the first to introduce syncopated music in Europe with an orchestra headed by Will Marion Cook. He has been Miss Dove's manager for ten years, having seen her possibilities when she was graduated with honors from the conservatory. Miss Dove has appeared in all of the European centers and played before the crown heads of Europe. While she is commonly referred to as the rival of Miss Baker, she really holds the same exalted position in Central Europe that Miss Baker holds in Paris. It was not until recently that the two stars crossed when Miss Dove succeeded the countess at the Casino de Paris in Paris. Prior to this Miss Dove had been the sensation of Vienna, Berlin, Copenhagen and Southern Italy. Miss Dove wears on her delicately tapered fingers tipped with vermilion, a simple wedding band which she refuses to discuss further than to say "It's just a protection against mashers." Asked if she had any ambitions toward marrying a count or any other member of royalty, she smiled gaily and answered: "I have no prejudice against counts—provided they are genuine, and I believe your American slang expression for that remark would be meow!" "If you find out anything about that wedding band more than she has told you," said Mr Lattimore, "you will do more than I have been able to learn in the past ten years." Miss Dove declared that she was wild about Harlem. Asked if she had seen so many colored people before all in one place, she added quickly, "Only in Africa." The most amazing thing of her American experiences, she said, is seeing colored men and women having a good time together and enjoying each other's company. She also enjoys American food and the high living scale. She loves Sugar Hill.

Some months later a further report in *The Afro American* (8 August 1936) revealed that, like Josephine Baker, Evelyn had difficulty winning over white American audiences who resisted her European charms and sophistication. Perhaps Evelyn took a risk by appearing at Connie's Inn, a nightclub, instead of a concert hall where she could have performed spirituals. Here is a transcript of the article, headlined "So the Bronze Dove Flies Back to Paris":

Miss Evelyn Dove, British-born song bird, who took a flyer in American theatricals last winter when she appeared at Connie's Inn on Broadway. She is back in Paris, where she made her biggest success, being none too pleased with America after her four-month experience. Like Josephine Baker, she dashed back to the continent the moment her engagement ended, and will have nothing more to do with this side of the ocean. "America", she laments, "does not want to see colored artists do anything of an artistic or cultured nature. Colored stars here are expected only to do 'swing stuff.'" Miss Dove studied at the best music conservatories on the continent and sings in many languages. She finds European audiences do not seem surprised when she renders a classic of the various nationalities in a night club, but American audiences take a different attitude. Miss Dove was also peeved with the racial restrictions to which she had never been accustomed.

Evelyn's appearance at Connie's Inn was a "first" for a black British female singer. Unless other names come to light, Evelyn is the pioneer. Since the Victorian era, many African American female artistes had crossed the North Atlantic Ocean to perform in Britain. One of the earliest was the concert singer Elizabeth Taylor Greenfield who, on a tour of England in 1854, sang for Queen Victoria at Buckingham Palace. In the Edwardian era there was Aida Overton Walker with the *In Dahomey* stage company and Belle Davis, who became a popular star of British music halls. In 1938 the British-born Mabel Mercer (see Chapter 3) made her New York debut as a cabaret singer with a six-month engagement at the Ruban Bleu Club, but Evelyn was the first.

Chapter 8: Cabaret Queen in India

Evelyn Dove loved to travel and the 1920s and 1930s took the London-born singer to such faraway places as Germany, France, Italy and the United States. She travelled to India to star in a cabaret show at the Harbour Bar in Bombay (now Mumbai, the official name since 1995), the capital city of the Indian state of Maharashtra. The Harbour Bar, situated in the Taj Mahal Palace and Tower Hotel, opened its doors in 1933, but the Taj hotel had existed for many years. Having opened in 1903, by the time it celebrated its centenary in 2003, it had survived two world wars and a big explosion in the docks in the 1930s which shook the building.

The Taj is still to this day located in the Mumbai harbour, close to the Gateway of India which was also known as the gateway of the country in the days of steamship travel. It was the point of all entries and exits from not just the city, but the entire country during the early years of the 20th century. The Taj witnessed remarkable events including the exit of the empire, when Lord Louis Mountbatten made his farewell speech before he left for England and the last ship, the *Somerset Lighton*, sailed out in 1947. The Taj was also where ballroom dancing in India was born, and in the 1960s the Beatles stayed there, as did the Oscar winning Hollywood actor Gregory Peck, whose bed at the hotel had to be lengthened to fit his 6ft 3in height. In addition to Evelyn, many entertainers and musicians performed at the Harbour Bar. For instance, in the 1930s there was a singer called Amy Denton who made an impression, and she is mentioned in an unidentified press cutting dated October 1937 in Evelyn's scrapbook. It reveals that the Harbour Bar was meant to be patronised by men only:

So Amy Denton came and the amazing part of the story is that women poured into the Harbour Bar. There was something about Amy that women were fascinated by. Tall, slender and defiant, with the voice of Tallulah and the will of Delilah, she sang her songs and told her daily tale. Outside men waited for a seat in that Harbour Bar. They waited, like so many Samsons, only too glad to be shorn. She came, she conquered and she left. She cannot be forgotten—she had that something.

During the Second World War Amy Denton, still living in Bombay, scandalised the local community when her boyfriend was arrested for being a German spy and she was also thought to be one.

The same unidentified press cutting continues:

Now Evelyn Dove is here. She is superb, in any way you care to think of. Face and figure, voice and melody. She has everything, has Evelyn Dove. You see her and you hear her sing and you are taken back to a front row seat watching "Blackbirds". Or the Cotton Club or Connie's Inn. Or just anywhere in New York or Paris between midnight and the milkman. I recollect that when the first coloured show came to London, years ago, there were more Rolls-Royces at the stage door than ever had been the case before. And since Evelyn Dove has come to thrill us at the Harbour Bar the quality of automobiles has greatly improved around the Taj. She sings a song in Spanish, and champagne is the only drink possible. She holds us with a spiritual and another cork goes pop. That is what she does, this lady who induces luxury out of melody.

Cabaret in India (1937)
from Evelyn's scrapbook

When Evelyn was due to open at the Taj on 6 October 1937, she was described by a columnist in *The Evening News of India* as:

...an artist of international reputation, one of the leading personalities of Europe's entertainment world and when she appeared on Broadway was one of the major sensations there. She is described as the closest rival of Josephine Baker herself. Born in London—her father is a wealthy barrister and practising on the Gold Coast. She made her first public appearance at the Wintergarten, Berlin under the direction of George Lattimore at the same time as Josephine Baker was introduced to an astounded Paris by Louis Douglas at the Champs Elysées. Since then these two coloured stars have dominated the variety and revue stages of Europe. Recently she replaced Josephine Baker in the latter's last revue at the Casino de Paris and was featured as a rival attraction at Connie's Inn, the famous New York resort, when Miss Baker was the star turn at the Ziegfeld Follies. Sounds good doesn't she? I hear she is every bit as good, and she isn't the Harlem brand either, so don't look for hotcha stuff or those mammy mannerisms from this brilliant entertainer who has been described as "the bronze toast of Paris and London" and "England's most beautiful creole". She wears a wedding ring, but she wouldn't tell me a thing about it except that "it's just a protection against mashers".

Evelyn was a sensation on her opening night, captivating audiences with her superb cabaret act in which she demonstrated her versatility. According to a journalist on *The Evening News of India* she included in her repertoire at least twelve songs, in English, French, Italian and German. These included "Love for Sale", Cole Porter's street walker's lament, which had been sung by Elisabeth Welch in the Broadway revue *The New Yorkers* in 1931. The song was considered too risqué for Broadway and some critics attacked Porter for lyrics they considered "filthy". Porter was so hurt by the criticisms that he left New York for Paris in a rage three days after the revue opened. In Britain the song was banned by the BBC and consequently it was not sung on the radio for many years. For Elisabeth Welch "Love for Sale" was "beautiful poetry because it was like one of the street cries of London." Elisabeth kept it in her repertoire until she retired in the 1990s. At the Harbour Bar, Evelyn also included in her act Josephine Baker's "theme song" "Les Deux Amours", Harry Warren and Al Dubin's beautiful and haunting "September in the Rain" and the lively spiritual "Gospel Train". Also on stage was Teddy Weatherford, the African American jazz pianist and an accomplished stride pianist who, in the 1920s, had worked with such jazz giants as Louis Armstrong. Weatherford had been leading a band at the Taj Mahal Hotel since the early 1930s. During the Second World War he led a band in Calcutta where he made radio broadcasts for the American Armed Forces Radio Service. He died of cholera in Calcutta in 1945 at the age of forty-one.

Evelyn's appearance was enthusiastically reviewed in "The Bombay Man's Diary" in *The Evening News of India* on 7 October 1937 and a copy of this was pasted in her scrapbook:

Well, Evelyn Dove put herself over in the very biggest way at that Harbour Bar last night. There's no question about it at all, the woman is a thorough artist to her finger tips, perfectly groomed, very very easy on the eye with her splendid, tall figure and her pleasant face and flashing eyes, and amazingly accomplished. We haven't had or heard anything quite like her in Bombay ever and it doesn't need a prophet to tell that she is liable to be the old burg's rage as long as she is there. It was a dreadful place for the debut of an artist. However, that didn't stop it from being the merriest, jolliest, and, yes, "bingyest" assembly I've ever known or heard of in Bombay. Near three hundred of the city's gayest spirits inside and I should think nearer a thousand that knocked but couldn't enter, because there just wasn't any room in the place even to stand them up. Teddy Weatherford got the big hand, bigger than both his together, when he bobbed his gladness to be back in Bombay and added a few words to express it. And then he rolled his hands at the piano and put over all the newest and the oldest stuff and generally got us ready for the titbit of the evening. Evelyn Dove didn't get just the big hand. She got an ovation, a roaring welcome that must have sent all the fish scuttling in terror out of the harbour just outside. Everybody I meet keeps asking me Is she like Amy Denton? My answer to that is the favourite of the ministers—the question simply does not arise. They belong to different worlds. Evelyn Dove made three appearances last night and sang at least twelve songs— English, French, Italian and German. She got off the mark perfectly with "Love for Sale" into which she put an amazing amount of wicked expression and then she sang "Les Deux Amours", "September in the Rain", the lively spiritual "Gospel Train", and another French ditty. I think it was "Parle d'amour Mario". Each revealed a different personality and through all there ran the confident ease of a practised artist to whom crowds and enthusiasm are nothing new. She was somewhat restrained, too. But definitely entertaining.

Chapter 9: Variety

The Coronation of Queen Elizabeth II in 1953 boosted the popularity of television hugely and it spread to over 50% of the population. A second channel, ITV, began broadcasting in 1955 and by the 1960s television was the main source of entertainment for the masses. Until then one of the main sources of entertainment had been the music hall, but television replaced it. Music halls, or "variety", provided a type of entertainment that had found popularity in the early Victorian era, and involved a mixture of popular songs, comedy and speciality acts. Evelyn started working in music halls early on in her career, but it was not until her return to Britain in 1938, a year before the outbreak of the Second World War, that she returned to the British variety stage.

When Evelyn started working in music halls she joined a select group of black women who had been entertaining in Britain since the nineteenth century. During Queen Victoria's reign (1837–1901), though many thousands of black people were living in Britain, the main contact white Britons had with people of African descent was either in sport (boxing) or in entertainment (music halls). One of the earliest known black women on the British stage was the American singer Amy Height. Born in Boston, Massachusetts about 1866, she began touring British music halls and appearing in Christmas pantomimes in the 1880s. In 1886, when she was featured in the pantomime *Robinson Crusoe* at the Grand Theatre in Islington, London, *The Stage* (31 December) noted that she "displays considerable humorous power and command of expression, whilst in the vocalisation of her songs she uses a clear and musical organ with considerable skill and effect." Amy continued working until she died in 1913 but her success was unusual for a black woman in Britain at that time. The British public's contact with black women was minimal in the Victorian and Edwardian eras, but the versatile Amy helped to break down barriers for black women in show business, including another African American, Belle Davis. Born in Chicago in 1874, from 1901 Belle spent most of her adult life in Europe, mostly Britain. Belle successfully toured the music halls of London and the provinces throughout the Edwardian era, and the First World War. Amy Height and Belle Davis were trailblazers who helped open the door for many other black women to have careers in music halls. Evelyn was part of a generation of British-born black women to achieve success in this field. Others included Mabel Mercer and Pep Graham.

After returning to Britain from her European and American adventures, Evelyn did not encounter any problems finding work on the variety stage. From contemporary reviews, Evelyn presented herself as a sophisticated and glamorous singer, whose repertoire combined popular songs, like "Can't Help Lovin' That Man", sung by the mixed-race character Julie La Verne who passes for white in the musical *Show Boat*, and spirituals. By scanning the pages of the entertainment journals *The Era* and *The Stage*, it has been possible to list off some of Evelyn's many appearances, and also to identify other black stars who were popular in variety at that time. For example, in *The Era* (8 December 1938), Evelyn is listed on the bill at the Dover Hippodrome. Other black acts listed included the comedy duo Scott and Whaley in *Chinese Follies of 1939* at the Empire, Edinburgh; the sophisticated singer/pianist Turner Layton at the Empire, Newcastle and his counter-part Leslie 'Hutch' Hutchinson at the New Cross Empire; and the popular Ken 'Snakehips' Johnson and his black British swing band at the Bristol Hippodrome. In 1938 and 1939 these artistes were among the elite of black British show business, and Evelyn was part of that group. Their popularity

with British audiences would continue into the Second World War.

Throughout 1939 Evelyn appeared at the Empress, Brixton; Shepherd's Bush Empire; Palace, Blackpool with Tom Walls; New Hippodrome, Manchester with Senor Wences, Tessie O'Shea, Dorothy Squires and Dick Henderson; Walthamstow Palace, London; Kings, Preston and the Palace, Southampton. When Evelyn appeared on the bill at London's popular Hackney Empire, *The Era* (17 August 1939) noted that she was "a beautifully sweet singer of whom more should be heard" and further praise awaited her when she appeared at the Theatre Royal, Dublin with Issy Bonn. *The Stage* (7 September 1939) singled her out: "An attractive stage show is provided here which includes Evelyn Dove, who delights her hearers with her pleasing personality and charming voice."

In 1939 and 1940, Evelyn's "pleasing personality and charming voice" was captured on several 78 rpm recordings, her first since the 1920s. On 27 October 1939 she recorded Cole Porter's "My Heart Belongs to Daddy" with Billy Cotton and his Band. In 1939 Cotton was one of the top band leaders in the country. Another top bandleader, Louis Levy, who was also well-known as a film composer and music director, utilised Evelyn's vocal talents on three of his popular "film selection" recordings: *Gulliver's Travels* (December 1939), *Babes in Arms* (January 1940), in which she sang Richard Rodgers and Lorenz

Hart's emotive "Where or When", and *Band Wagon* (1940). There were also recordings of Harold Arlen and E. Y. Harburg's Oscar winning "Over the Rainbow", and an emotional wartime hit by Roy King and Stanley Hill called "I'll Pray for You", which was also popularised by Vera Lynn.

By the time the war broke out on 3 September 1939, Evelyn had become a firm favourite with music hall audiences and this continued throughout the war, helped by her BBC Radio fame. From 1939 to 1945 her war service included entertaining the troops as noted by the entertainment journal *Variety* in March 1941. On Sunday 9 March Evelyn took part in a show for troops and defence workers at the Scala Theatre. Scott and Whaley were also on the bill, but another act, Ken 'Snakehips' Johnson and his West Indian Dance Orchestra, did not appear. The previous evening Ken and several band members had been killed when a bomb destroyed the Café de Paris where they were performing. One can only imagine what was going through Evelyn's mind when she took to the stage of the Scala Theatre that evening. Just one month had passed since Evelyn and Ken had broadcast to the nation in BBC Radio's 'Services Spotlight' segment of *Sunday Matinee* on 9 February. At the end of the war, Evelyn readily agreed to take part in some of the *Victory Shows for the Forces* organised by the *News of the World* newspaper. A programme for one of these shows—staged on 13 May 1945 at the Adelphi Theatre in London's Strand—is pasted in her scrapbook. Top of the bill was the popular music hall comedian Max Miller, popularly known as the 'Cheeky Chappie'. On 22 October 1942 Evelyn is listed in *The Stage* as a member of a variety unit under Theatres War Service Council. In 1945 Evelyn made her debut in a traditional Christmas pantomime.

Evelyn's scrapbook also includes newspaper reviews in which she is singled out and praised.

Here is a selection of some of the newspaper reviews relating to her appearances in variety theatres up and down the country:

At the Palace Theatre, Huddersfield:

There is something to please everyone in the show at the Palace Theatre this week. It is a good all-round holiday programme, and the acts of jugglers, the trick cyclists and acrobats are especially suitable for children. Evelyn Dove is well-known for her type of vocalism, and she proved very popular with audiences last night. She sings not popular songs but those which are well enough known to be appreciated. There were one or two Negro spirituals which she sang very pleasingly. (*Huddersfield Daily Examiner*, 27 April 1943)

At the Grand Theatre, Brighton:

Some of the brightest and most enjoyable interludes at the Grand Theatre this week are those featuring the attractive Continental singer, Evelyn Dove, with Harry Groombridge and his Hot Quintette. Harry and his Boys certainly know how to put over a number in the very latest style, while Evelyn Dove—a striking personality with dark, glistening hair, and wide, expressive eyes—sings at the microphone in a manner that is as attractive as it is somehow "different". Evelyn Dove does more than just sing her songs. She imparts to them an emotional depth which gives her soft voice an added pleasantness. An excellent musical background is provided by the Quintette, which also proves most effective in the rendering of modern swing tunes. (*Brighton Herald*, 24 July 1943)

At the Halifax Palace, Halifax:

Evelyn Dove shows charming personality in her singing of some beautiful songs, including negro spirituals. (*Halifax Daily Courier*, 10 August 1943)

Another vocalist of merit is Evelyn Dove, who combines a charming personality with tuneful music. (*Brighouse Echo*, 13 August 1943)

At the Palace, Newscastle:

Stars of the Orient, an unusual show featuring the talented Young China Troupe and those famous stage stars Evelyn Dove and Walter Niblo. The programme is full of original speciality acts. (*Newcastle Sunday Sun*, 23 April 1944)

At the Royalty Theatre, Cheshire:

Original and invigorating variety of a high standard is staged this week at the Royalty Theatre, each act characterised by exceptional merit. The BBC coloured songstress, Evelyn Dove, sings with soothing richness of voice and personality such as well-chosen numbers as "Can't Help Lovin' That Man", "Stormy Weather" and "Mighty Like a Rose" (in which "Smilin' Thro" is discriminately interpolated). (*Cheshire Observer*, 24 June 1944)

At the Grand Theatre, Brighton:

The undoubted star of *Foolish Things* at the Grand Theatre, Brighton is Evelyn Dove, the singer who is broadcasting weekly in *Serenade in Sepia*. Negroid songs, ideally suited to her rich contralto voice, are her speciality and her repertoire includes "Jonah and the Whale", "Shadrack" and "Mighty Like a Rose". (*Sussex Daily News*, 18 September 1945)

Foolish Things is a bright and lively show, topical, humorous and tuneful... Evelyn Dove, the star of *Serenade in Sepia*, sings delightfully. (*The Stage*, 20 September 1945)

There are many attractive features in the new show *Foolish Things* at the Grand Theatre this week... Evelyn Dove, the star of radio's *Serenade in Sepia*, scores a great success with her songs. (*Brighton Herald*, 22 September 1945)

At the Alexandra Theatre, Birmingham:

Evelyn Dove, who plays the Queen of Cantata in *Dick Whittington* at the Alexandra Theatre, Birmingham, resumes her partnership with Edric Connor when *Serenade in Sepia* returns to the air on 3 February. It will be broadcast without change of cast at three o'clock on Sunday afternoons and Miss Dove will go to London for each performance. It is difficult to realise that the artist who tells the story of Belshazzar's Feast in the pantomime is she who so extended one's knowledge of negro spirituals. (*Birmingham Mail*, 30 January 1946)

At the Pier Pavilion, Worthing:

RADIO STAR SHINES. Evelyn Dove, the singing star of the radio show *Serenade in Sepia*, and Herbert Thorpe, the well-known operatic tenor, were the soloists at the Pier Pavilion on Sunday evening. Miss Dove sang a number of characteristic songs, outstanding among them being "Can't Help Lovin' That Man", Stephen Foster's evergreen "I Dream of Jeannie With the Light Brown Hair", "Deep River" and "Water Boy". (*Worthing Gazette*, 28 August 1946)

Chapter 10: BBC Radio

After launching its radio service in 1922, the British Broadcasting Corporation, popularly known as the BBC, provided both news and entertainment for its listeners, at home and overseas. The BBC quickly gained a reputation for being stuffy and old-fashioned and was known as "Auntie" because it had a reputation for being prim and prissy. However, in spite of this image, in its early, formative years, the 1920s and 1930s and throughout the Second World War, the BBC was arguably more culturally diverse than it is given credit for. For example, the BBC showcased a number of black singers and musicians in their broadcasts and, as early as 1934, Elisabeth Welch was prominently featured in the radio series *Soft Lights and Sweet Music*. In 1937, at the height of his popularity in Britain, Paul Robeson was voted the most popular singer on BBC Radio. In the series *The American Half-Hour* (1935) Alistair Cooke devoted an entire programme to "The Negro". The *Radio Times* promised that Cooke would look at the "Negro" "as orator, poet, preacher, writer, composer, and singer." In Cooke's programme, poetry was represented by James Weldon Johnson and music by Duke Ellington and W. C. Handy. In 1939

Ken 'Snakehips' Johnson, the popular Guyanese leader of Britain's first black "swing" band, presented a programme about black Caribbean music called *Calypso and other West Indian Music*.

During the war, black singers were prominently featured and female vocalists like Evelyn, Elisabeth Welch, Ida Shepley and Adelaide Hall were regularly employed by the BBC in a range of music and variety programmes such as *Monday Night at Eight*, *Variety Bandbox*, *Starlight*, and *Workers' Playtime*. In 1943 Adelaide had her own series *Wrapped in Velvet*. In May 1945, during the Victory in Europe celebrations, the African American entertainer Josephine Baker visited London and took part in several victory shows and BBC broadcasts. The same artistes could also be heard on the BBC's Empire Service in such programmes as *Calling the West Indies* and *Calling West Africa*. However, in 1925, Evelyn was one of the pioneers of radio broadcasting and, until other examples can be found, she can be claimed to be the first black woman to broadcast on BBC Radio. The second would be Mabel Mercer, also in 1925. The African American contralto, Marian Anderson, made a number of broadcasts for the

BBC in recitals from 1928 and during subsequent visits to Britain.

Evelyn began broadcasting for the BBC as early as 25 May 1925, just a few years after the corporation launched its service. Listeners were restricted to the London area and Evelyn was featured in a programme called *Negro Melodies* as a member of The Southern Trio. The other two members of the Trio were John Payne and C.C. (Clinton) Rosemond. On 4 July 1925 The Southern Trio were featured in the "Negro Melodies" segment of *Independence Day*, described in the *Radio Times* as "a programme for American listeners" who were based in London. The Southern Trio, with Evelyn, made a further appearance in *Way Down South* (16 July 1925) before she left for Europe and *The Chocolate Kiddies* revue (see Chapter 4). Mabel Mercer took her place in the Trio and appeared with them in a BBC Radio broadcast that had been originally scheduled for Evelyn, *Variety* (19 September 1925).

Evelyn spent many years travelling abroad and did not return to the BBC and radio broadcasting until 30 January 1939 when she made a guest appearance in *Monday Night at Seven*. Evelyn then joined the African American baritone Rollin Smith for *Mississippi Nights* (26 March 1939), with the BBC Theatre Orchestra conducted by Stanford Robinson. The programme was described in the *Radio Times* as one that will "present Negro music in varying moods" and Evelyn was described as a singer who has had "many successes in New York and on the Continent." Later that year, Evelyn was given her own music series, *Sweet and Lovely* which began broadcasting on 15 November 1939, just after the outbreak of war, and continued until 28 December.

By studying production files at the BBC's Written Archives, more detailed information about Evelyn's early wartime broadcasts reveals the types of programmes that featured her, and the songs that were selected for her to sing. Mostly, Evelyn broadcast in radio shows that used her gifts as a cabaret singer. One of the songs Evelyn regularly featured was Jerome Kern and Oscar Hammerstein II's famous torch song "Can't Help Lovin' That Man" from the musical *Show Boat*. In *Dance Cabaret* (13 January, 1940) she sang "Can't Help Lovin' That Man" as well as "Goodnight, My Beautiful" and "I'll See You in My Dreams". The *Radio Times* often described her as "The Girl With the Golden Voice". Another famous torch song performed by Evelyn in a later *Dance Cabaret* broadcast (17 July 1940) was George and Ira Gershwin's "The Man I Love". In that same programme she also sang the popular wartime hit, Eric Maschwitz and Manning Sherwin's romantic love song "A Nightingale Sang in Berkeley Square". In *Cabaret (For the Forces)* (8 March 1941), Evelyn included Jerome Kern and Oscar Hammerstein II's nostalgic (and Oscar winning) "The

December 16

767 kc/s 391.1 m. and 668 kc/s 449.1 m.

SATURDAY

Here is Evelyn Dove, the British coloured singer who has starred all over the world. She broadcasts on Saturday in 'Sweet and Lovely'.

5.30 **'SWEET AND LOVELY'**

A musical presentation by
Peter Yorke and his Orchestra
with Evelyn Dove, Sam Browne

Presented by Douglas Lawrence

6.0 **Time Signal, Greenwich: NEWS**

'RHAPSODY IN BLACK.' (Left to right) Roy Speer, who produces another of these popular shows of 'music in ebony' this afternoon at 4.20, at a studio rehearsal with Elisabeth Welch, Frisco, and Evelyn Dove.

Sweet and Lovely (BBC 1940) from Evelyn's scrapbook

WEDNESDAY Home Service

JUNE 19   1013 kc/s   296.2 m.   767 kc/s   391.1 m.   668 kc/s   449.1 m.

4.20 ' RHAPSODY IN BLACK '—1

Music in ebony from Harlem to
Savannah
with
Elizabeth Welch, Frisco, Evelyn Dove,
Malmaison, the Georgia Crackers, the
BBC Revue Orchestra, conducted by
Hyam Greenbaum

Script by the compère, James Dyrenforth. Produced by Roy Speer

Elizabeth Welch by the warm colour
of her voice has endeared herself to
listeners. Born in New York City,
she was singing at nine years old.
She sang in a church choir, a glee
club, and a quartet, then found her
way to the theatre. She met Caleb
Porter ; met him again in Paris,
and he said: ' I've a song for you.'
She sang ' Solomon ' at the *Bœuf-
sur-le-Toit* and then at *Chez
Florence.* Then C. B. Cochran
engaged her for *Nymph Errant* at
the Duke of York's Theatre, London,
and she never looked back. She won
radio fame in ' Soft Lights and
Sweet Music '.

Evelyn Dove, London-born and
as lovely a coloured singer as ever
broadcast, was a student at the Royal
Academy of Music, studying singing
and music. Then she went abroad.
She has performed in no fewer than
nineteen countries, and made a great
hit in cabaret at Connie's Inn, New
York. She was a radio favourite in
the States. Two years ago she came
to England to win radio fame over
here.

Frisco was the name given to
Joscelyn Bingham, also a coloured
artist, when he drew crowds
wherever he appeared in San Fran-
cisco. He came to Europe and added
to his fame, not only as an artist
but as a club proprietor. ' Frisco's ',
both in Paris and London, became
famous. He last appeared on the
stage in Erik Charell's production of
The Merry Widow in Berlin before
the days when Hitler was to take
everything merry from that city.

5.0 NEWYDDION (News in Welsh)

Mike	Jack Melford
Penny	Patricia Leonard
Angel	Marion Wilson
' Props '	Jacques Brown
Roddy	Sam Costa

4.20 ' RHAPSODY IN BLACK '—1
Music in ebony
(*See Home Service*)

' RHAPSODY IN BLACK '. Elizabeth Welch (left) and Evelyn Dove,
whom you will hear this afternoon at 4.20 singing in the first show of this
new weekly series of songs from Harlem to Savannah.

Rhapsody in Black (BBC 1940) from Evelyn's scrapbook

Last Time I Saw Paris" which had been inspired by the fall of France to the Nazis in 1940. In another edition of *Cabaret* (11 August 1941), Evelyn sang Cole Porter's haunting "Night and Day" and in *Starlight (For the Forces)* (28 January 1942) she sang Vincent Youmans, Billy Rose and Edward Eliscu's beautiful "Without a Song". In addition to the many cabaret programmes, Evelyn was also invited by the BBC to sing spirituals. On 25 September 1941 she took part in an uplifting and inspiring programme for the troops called *Negro Spirituals (For the Forces)* in which she sang, among others, "Deep River", "Nobody Knows the Trouble I See" and "Were You There?".

The BBC's Empire Service, which has been known as the BBC World Service since 1965, began in December 1932. Its broadcasts were mainly aimed at English speakers in the outposts of the British Empire or, as King George V put it in the first-ever Royal Christmas Message, the "men and women, so cut off by the snow, the desert, or the sea, that only voices out of the air can reach them." Radio came to the British Caribbean in the 1930s and the war helped develop radio broadcasting in the region. It was used to relay news of the war and to boost morale. Those radio stations relied heavily on the United States radio networks or the BBC for news and entertainment programmes. The BBC's Empire Service helped enormously in this respect, with

programmes like *Calling the West Indies* proving very successful. In addition to providing news, *Calling the West Indies* featured guests from all walks of life, as well as singers like Evelyn.

One of the most influential black people at the BBC in wartime was the Jamaican feminist, poet, playwright, and social activist Una Marson. In 1939 she accepted an offer from Cecil Madden, a BBC producer, to undertake some freelance work and this gave Una a stepping-stone into the organisation. Consequently she became the BBC's first black woman programme maker and presenter. Una's pioneering work for BBC Radio spanned just over five years (1940–45). On 3 March 1941 Una was appointed as full-time programme assistant on the BBC's Empire Service and through the weekly series *Calling the West Indies*, Una was able to send messages from servicemen and women in England to their families and friends in the West Indies. Listeners throughout the Caribbean would gather in front of their radios, sometimes up to three times a week, to listen to *Calling the West Indies*. In spite of air raids, at their worst during the London Blitz (September 1940 to May 1941), and other wartime risks, although it was dangerous broadcasting from a BBC studio Una and her guests, including Evelyn, understood the importance and value of *Calling the West Indies*.

Throughout the war, black musicians and entertainers could be heard in a range of morale-boosting BBC music shows. BBC Radio also launched the British career of the Trinidadian folk singer (and folk hero) Edric Connor. In the early post-war years, Edric became a major celebrity on BBC Radio and television, and a much-loved and respected ambassador for the arts and culture of the Caribbean. From 1945 to 1947 one of the radio and television programmes that boosted his popularity was *Serenade in Sepia*, in which he co-starred with Evelyn, just a few months after they had worked together in a programme called *Round the World in Song* (8 February 1945). On 31 December 1946 Evelyn and Edric teamed up for a BBC Radio version of *Song of the South*, based on the popular Walt Disney musical film then on release. In this highly romanticised vision of America's 'Old South' featuring the stories of Brer Rabbit, Edric starred as the storyteller Uncle Remus and Evelyn was cast as Aunt Tempy.

In the 1930s Edric Connor worked as a mechanical engineer while in his spare time he researched and studied Caribbean folk music. He was also a trained baritone. During the early part of the war he worked on the construction of the American naval air base in Trinidad and saved enough money to travel to Britain. He left Trinidad in December 1943 and on his arrival in London in February 1944 he took a job working in a munitions factory in London's East End. He didn't stay there for very long. He had already presented a series about Caribbean folk music on Radio Trinidad, and on his journey to Britain he carried with him some notes on Caribbean folk music, including calypso, as well as letters of introduction to the BBC. Two weeks after his arrival he made his debut on BBC Radio in *Calling the West Indies* for the Empire Service. He also took part in *Tribute to the King* with a group of representatives of the British Commonwealth and Empire. This was broadcast immediately before the King George VI's speech on VE Day, 8 May 1945.

Edric's appealing voice and charming personality made a deep impression on listeners. His widow, Pearl Connor-Mogotsi, also from Trinidad, told me in 1993:

Towards the end of the war, and immediately after, the British government made an effort to show some appreciation for all the people from the colonies who had contributed to the war effort. Those little Caribbean islands had all stuck their necks on the block. Some of our young men had gone and died. My own brother joined the Royal Air Force and flew a Lancaster bomber. So the British government wanted to show some appreciation. There was an open-door policy. They weren't locking us out yet. But it didn't last. The BBC was also interested in helping to promote and assist some of the third-world people

With Edric Connor in *Serenade in Sepia* (1945)
Courtesy of BBC

Serenade in Sepia (1945)
Courtesy of BBC

and the Caribbean people. So Edric came to Britain at a good time. Doors were open to him. He didn't have to kick too hard.

Serenade in Sepia was a music programme devised by the radio producer Eric Fawcett in which Evelyn and Edric sang spirituals, folk songs and popular songs accompanied by Eugene Pini and his Orchestra. It was described in the *Radio Times* as a programme of "sweet music in the Negro style" and was due to be launched on 8 May 1945, but a major event led to the postponement of the first broadcast. Edric recalled in his autobiography, *Horizons – The Life and Times of Edric Connor*, published posthumously in 2007: "The day the war in Europe ended (May 8 1945), Eric Fawcett, Evelyn and I were to broadcast the first instalment of a new series of programmes called *Serenade in Sepia*. Our work was postponed so that the BBC could do justice to the occasion. Nevertheless we recorded the programme. Most public transport stopped running. Housewives left kitchens. Shops and schools were closed. All commercial and industrial activities ceased. The only way I could get to London that day was in a hearse. As I sat near the coffin I contemplated the dead body it contained. What a day to go. Then I thought of the millions of people killed in the war and wept quietly. Somebody had to cry for the

steel that is bent and the body broken against its will. Somebody has to cry for the children unborn and those born but hungry. Somebody has to cry for humanity. They put me down at Oxford Circus."

Serenade in Sepia was recorded on 8 May and eventually broadcast for the first time on Friday 11 May 1945 at 9.30 in the evening. Edric Connor said: "*Serenade in Sepia* was an immediate success. After the second week the option was taken up for a further eight programmes. The pall and dust of war hung grimly over London. All eyes were turned to Burma and the Far East. Chipped and cracked cups were used in the best restaurants. At the BBC and elsewhere we stirred tea with the handle of a fork, a makeshift that becomes a habit. A universal habit. The orchestra we had in *Serenade in Sepia* were the best musicians in the world and all had their own orchestras. But we looked forward to working together once a week. We certainly had a lot of fun. We knew we were doing something good."

Serenade in Sepia was an immediate success with radio listeners, worn down by the war, facing an uncertain future. They warmed to the intimacy and lovely singing of Evelyn and Edric. Their fan mail was enormous and the series ran on the BBC's Home Service for forty-five weeks with one repeat at home and five repeats overseas and throughout the world. From 31 July 1945 the series was broadcast under a different title, *Let My People Sing* on the Empire Service, enabling listeners to hear Evelyn and Edric on the North American Service (including the Caribbean), African Service and The General Forces Programme. Photographs of Evelyn and Edric were published in the *Radio Times* and *London Calling*, the BBC's journal for the Empire Service. For over two years, until its final broadcast on 20 September 1947, Evelyn and Edric were two of BBC Radio's most popular singing personalities. Edric reflected: "I worked hard. I was famous. My programme was a success."

Press reports were enthusiastic and Evelyn kept two press cuttings about the series in her scrapbook. The *Daily Mail* (13 September 1945) raved: "Evelyn Dove and Edric Connor, in *Serenade in Sepia* (inspired title), can, so far as I am concerned, go on forever. This is a first rate BBC effort and should thus be put to credit account. I tremble lest this show becomes too popular, for then they will take it off. Nothing recedes like success." The *Evening News* (5 October 1945) ran a story about the programme, and featured a photograph of Evelyn:

By planning in advance a programme based on detailed returns of listeners' preferences, the BBC have produced one of their most popular features. *Serenade in Sepia*, the negro-style music programme, with coloured singers Evelyn Dove and Edric Connor, was prepared after Eric Fawcett, the producer, had studied the Listeners' Research figures gathered from all over the country about other musical shows, such as *Grand Hotel* and *Thursday Serenade*. He found that listeners liked announcements in one block, that they preferred a certain type of programme-building, and that they liked to hear Edric Connor talk as well as sing. These and many other points were incorporated. Now a large fan mail reaches the stars, with requests for repetitions of West Indian negro songs that Connor jotted down from a 95–year-old negro who was still working a few years ago in a plantation for 1s. 8d. a day rather than accept charity. Connor, who arrived in England last year and has broadcast here 20 times, was once a mechanical engineer. Evelyn Dove, born in England, made a hit in New York cabaret and has performed in 19 countries. *Serenade in Sepia* is heard on Sundays at 6.30pm and on Mondays at 4.45 in the Home Service.

Chapter 11: Evelyn and Elisabeth Welch

In 1940 the BBC brought Evelyn and Elisabeth Welch together for the popular radio series *Rhapsody in Black*. This began on 19 June 1940 and ran for twelve programmes, ending on 3 September. The *Radio Times* described the series as "music in ebony from Harlem to Savannah" and also featured several other British-based African American entertainers in support of Evelyn and Elisabeth. These included the veteran Norris Smith and Jocelyn 'Frisco' Bingham, who had been an expatriate nightclub owner in Paris before the war, and in 1940 owned the London nightclub Frisco's. The *Radio Times* launched the series by publishing photographs of Evelyn and Elisabeth.

In 1993 Elisabeth and I discussed Evelyn and their work for the BBC:

I sang in the Sunday school choir in my local church from the age of seven in New York, but Evelyn had a *trained* voice. She had top training at the Royal Academy of Music. She tried to be American, but was English. To be American in those days helped to get you work at the BBC and in variety. As singers we were in the same category; we were more or less based at the BBC. We were both *names* in radio. We were rivals, not enemies. The BBC would not usually hire me *and* Evelyn at the same time, though we did appear in *some* radio programmes together, like *Rhapsody in Black*. That's how I knew her. Before we worked together, I was a bigger name because I came from a background of cabaret and West End musicals, like Cole Porter's *Nymph Errant*, which was grand musical theatre, *not* variety! And Evelyn came from cabaret and variety. Evelyn wasn't loud or showy, like some Americans. The best description I can give is that she was a respectable middle-class English girl with a charming personality. She sang well, which made her perfect for broadcasting.

In 1940, when Evelyn and Elisabeth worked together, Elisabeth was having a "secret" relationship with the Honourable David Astor, a member of one of the world's wealthiest and most powerful families. Elisabeth's relationship with Astor, which lasted from 1935 to 1944, had to be kept a secret. His mother, the imperious and formidable Nancy, Viscountess Astor, was Britain's first female Member of Parliament, a Tory. David Astor had been educated at Eton and Oxford and had fallen in love with Elisabeth when he saw her in cabaret at London's famous

Café de Paris. She sang Cole Porter's "Love for Sale", and he was smitten. Nancy Astor had been raised in the American South, at a colonial mansion with a farm near Charlottesville, Virginia. Growing up, she had been affectionate towards the family's black servants, some of them former slaves. In spite of her background, her friends did not consider her a racist, but she disapproved of her son's relationship with Elisabeth. In Britain, mixed marriages were not against the law, as they were in many American States, but in certain social circles, notably Britain's upper classes, it was unthinkable for blacks and whites to marry. Even inter-racial affairs were frowned upon. In the 1930s Lady Edwina Mountbatten's extra-marital affair with the West Indian entertainer Leslie 'Hutch' Hutchinson had shocked "society". No wonder David and Elisabeth kept their relationship private.

Regarding their parentage, Evelyn and Elisabeth had something in common. They were the children of mixed marriages. Elisabeth was born in New York in 1904 to a father who was of African and Native American Indian heritage. Her mother was a white Scottish lass from Leith in Edinburgh. Elisabeth told me that when they wanted to be married in New York in 1902, "They found a Catholic priest who married them in secret. My mother was a wonderful woman. She was brave and defiant. I consider such marriage

natural, for love has no barriers and should not be hindered by laws."

I was made aware of a "liaison" between Elisabeth and David in 1993 when Adelaide Hall coyly shared this information. In hushed tones Adelaide told me that, when the war broke out, American ex-patriates were expected to return home: "Elisabeth stayed here because she was in love with David Astor and she didn't want to leave him, but it wasn't spoken about." In 2016 Jeremy Lewis barely mentioned the relationship in his biography of David Astor. He describes the young David—after he had left Oxford in 1934—as a young man who had turned against his family and social position. Lewis quotes Astor's brother Michael: "For a time he turned abruptly against his own class in society… I resented his experiments at living which seemed to disregard the fragile structure of our society." Jeremy explained to me that:

Elisabeth only gets two mentions in my book. I didn't come across a single mention of her in David Astor's own papers, or in other books and documents I consulted; and it's only thanks to you and to what you very kindly told me, that she gets into the book at all. I wish I could have given her more space. I'm sure you're right in suggesting that his family were embarrassed by the whole business—hence her being, as it were, written out of the story. I'm all for the story being more widely known.

Felix Inglis Allen,
Evelyn's second husband

After the war, David Astor married twice but Elisabeth never married. However, in 1964 she finally took the surname Astor, albeit a fictional one. Her friend Robert Gould wrote an original television musical for her, the enchanting *The Rise and Fall of Nellie Brown*. She played a "Broadway star who took London by storm" and the star's name was Lillabelle Astor.

A few months after working with Elisabeth, Evelyn married her second husband, Felix Allen, a white Lieutenant in the Royal Navy Volunteer Reserve. They were married at the Register Office in Bristol on 19 March 1941. Felix was the son of the Oxford-educated dramatist and humorist Henry Inglis Allen (1879–1943). Unlike Elisabeth and David, the Allens did not have to keep their marriage a secret. Sadly, the marriage did not last and ended in divorce in 1949 when Evelyn left for India. Felix's nephew, Jeremy Syers, takes up the story:

On my Uncle Felix Allen, I am not sure I can tell you much of particular interest. I did not see him a great deal until after the war when I was older and he came back to the UK for holidays; even then it was periodic. It was therefore mainly after he had separated from Evelyn Dove in 1949, whom I never met. He was with the Free French Navy during the war, when he was of course married to Evelyn Dove. He served with them throughout as far as I know. My grandmother was half-French. We were in South Africa from 1942 to 1946, so I did not see him at all then. After the war he went to West Africa where he worked for many years with a private import export business until he retired in 1962, and then he settled in Antigua where he knew one or two people, and spent a great deal of time painting, which was a hobby of his. He also opened a gift shop in St Johns, the capital of Antigua, with a friend. He owned one or two houses on a complex including his own. He came back to England periodically which was when we saw him. He was fond of light music and had a collection of Nat King Cole tapes among others, so obviously he enjoyed Evelyn's singing I would have thought. I greatly enjoyed his company and he was a great prankster and had a fund of jokes. He was very good company. He came back to England in 1979 and sadly died in hospital in London.

Felix Allen died at the age of seventy in St Bartholomew's Hospital, Smithfield, London on 5 June 1979.

Elisabeth Welch kept a silver framed photo of the young David Astor by her bedside until the day she died. Among Evelyn's possessions was a photographic studio portrait of Felix which she kept until she died. It was the only photograph she kept of any of her three husbands.

Chapter 12: BBC Television

On 2 November 1936 the talented African American double-act Buck and Bubbles made history when they took part in a variety show on the opening day of the BBC's high-definition television service at their Alexandra Palace studio in North London. The *Radio Times* described Buck and Bubbles as "a coloured pair who are versatile comedians who dance, play the piano, sing and cross-chat." They were the first of a succession of black entertainers and singers who made an important contribution to the early, formative years of British television. In those early days all television programmes were transmitted live, for just a few hours a day, to a limited audience which was exclusively white and middle-class. Also, between 1936 and 1939, before the outbreak of the Second World War interrupted the service, BBC Television could only be transmitted in the London area. It was an expensive commodity, costing the same as a new car, hence only the affluent could afford it.

Pre-war television showcased some of the greatest black personalities then working in Britain. Some of the African Americans had come to Europe in the 1920s and 1930s because they encountered less virulent racism and

more work. As the blues singer Alberta Hunter said: "In Europe they had our names up in lights. People in the United States would not give us that chance." In addition to Buck and Bubbles, who at the time of their 1936 appearance were starring in a West End revue called *Transatlantic Rhythm*, there was Paul Robeson, Adelaide Hall, the Mills Brothers and Fats Waller all making early television appearances for the BBC. Bruce Norman, author of *Here's Looking at You – The Story of British Television 1908–1939* (1984), says that, in the early, pre-war years of BBC Television, the programme emphasis was on entertainment and quoted one of BBC Television's earliest programme makers, Cecil Madden: "We had such frightfully good entertainment available to us. There were shows going on in all the London nightclubs... There was cabaret, an artist or two in every place... Of very high class. The sort of people we really wanted and so we were able to draw on a great deal of ready-made entertainment without having to do an awful lot of rehearsing ourselves." Among the "class acts" invited to Alexandra Palace in those early, pre-war years was Elisabeth Welch. She later described what being on television was

like for a singer: "At Alexandra Palace you had to climb over a whole sea of cables just to get to the camera which never moved, it was fixed to the floor, so you just stood there in front of it and sang your song. It was static, nerve-racking but amusing."

Evelyn was another "class act" and television pioneer. She made her first appearance in the new medium on 13 October 1938 in a popular daytime magazine programme called *Picture Page*, televised live from Alexandra Palace. Evelyn sang "Ma Lindy Lou" and was accompanied on piano by the black jazz pianist Yorke de Sousa. However, the outbreak of the Second World War interrupted the BBC's television service, and it was temporarily abandoned on 1 September 1939 when the screen simply

went blank. When the BBC reopened its television service after the war, on 7 June 1946, black artistes continued to be provided with work. A diverse range of singers, dancers and musicians were featured from 1946–1949 and these included African Americans such as the legendary entertainers Adelaide Hall and Josephine Baker, the opera singers Todd Duncan and Kenneth Spencer, and Katherine Dunham and her dance company. Caribbeans included the Jamaican trumpet soloist and bandleader Leslie 'Jiver' Hutchinson and the Trinidadian pianist Winifred Atwell. In 1947 the Jamaican string bassist Coleridge Goode took part in one of the first jazz programmes, *Jazz Is Where You Find It* and from West Africa came the West African Dunia who performed a Yoruba Tribal Dance from Nigeria. Sadly, before the existence of videotape, there was no technology to record any of these early appearances except telerecording, an expensive, rarely used process by which a live transmission could be filmed from a television screen.

On 22 June 1946 Edric Connor was the first black artiste to be featured on the BBC's post-war television service in *Music Makers*. Two days later on 24 June, Edric was featured again, this time in *Ballet Nègres*. This innovative programme also starred the black British dance company Ballet Nègres, led by the Jamaican Berto Pasuka, and the West African Rhythm Brothers. It was produced by Eric Fawcett who then cast Edric in a supporting role in the Eugene O'Neill drama *All God's Chillun' Got Wings*, shown on 16 September 1946. The Guyanese actor Robert Adams took the lead role as Jim Harris who falls in love with and marries a white woman. Adams also played the Prince of Morocco in a television version of William Shakespeare's *The Merchant of Venice* in 1947.

Eric Fawcett had been instrumental in bringing Edric Connor and Evelyn together for the highly successful radio series *Serenade in Sepia* (see Chapter 10) and when Fawcett began working more regularly in television, he decided to bring the series to Alexandra Palace. When the television version of *Serenade in Sepia* made its successful debut on Thursday 18 July 1946 at 3pm, repeated at 8.30pm, it made television stars out of Evelyn and Edric and they became the first black artistes to be given their own series in the new medium. Said Edric in his autobiography: "Now I didn't only have to sound good. I also had to look good."

Launching the series, the *Radio Times* (21 June 1946) described the series as a "sincerely beautiful presentation" that had "won a big following of listeners". They added that Evelyn and Edric had "made a highly photogenic picture in television tests at Alexandra Palace earlier this year. Eric Fawcett, the producer, will aim at presenting them in vision very much as they appeared in the broadcast studios, without the use of extravagant settings. One of the items will almost certainly be Edric Connor's sung version of 'The Lord's Prayer.'" In a later edition, the *Radio Times* (7 March 1947) said that the programme had:

undergone some rather subtle changes since it was first presented as a radio feature. It began as a sort of "soft lights and sweet music" programme, with songs ranging from lullabies to negro spirituals. Evelyn's deep contralto and Edric's resonant baritone voices blended to perfection, and it was not long before a considerable fan mail began to arrive— especially after Edric's rendering of his West Indian version of "The Lord's Prayer". Now, request items are a regular feature. From the pictorial viewpoint, *Serenade in Sepia* is regarded by those who should know as high-grade television.

Production files at the BBC's Written Archives confirm some of the songs Evelyn selected to perform in various editions. In the first programme Evelyn sang four songs: "Mighty Lak a Rose", "Porgy", "Shadrack" and "The Blind Man Stood in the Road and Cried". There followed "My Old Kentucky Home", "Kobee's Song", "Swing Along" and "Didn't It Rain" (3 April 1947); "Mississippi Mama", "Lil' Gal", "St Louis Blues" and "Couldn't Hear Nobody Pray", which Evelyn had recorded in the 1920s (11 April 1947); and "Sleepy Hills of Tennessee", "Ma Curly Headed Baby", "Happiness is a Thing Called Joe" from the musical *Cabin in the Sky* and the spiritual "Swing Low, Sweet Chariot" (27 June 1947). The series continued into 1947, with twelve thirty-minute programmes, plus repeats. It ended on 27 June 1947.

In addition to *Serenade in Sepia*, the two stars also worked for Eric Fawcett in two variety specials for BBC Television: *Variety in Sepia* (7 October 1947) and *Sepia* (1 December 1948). Both shows featured all-black casts, and a range of music. *Variety in Sepia* was transmitted live for one hour from Radiolympia at Earl's Court. It was broken down into five scenes, depicting the story of black song and dance down the years. Fawcett told the *Radio Times* (3 October 1947) that he intended to fill the show with the "best coloured talent in the country today." The final line-up included Edric, Evelyn (singing "Shadrack"), Buddy

Bradley, Winifred Atwell, Woods and Jarrett, Mable Lee, Cyril Blake and his Calypso Band, The Business Men of Rhythm, Vroom and his Dancers, and Adelaide Hall. The programme was transmitted twice, on 7 and 9 October. The transmission on 7 October has become significant to television history for the six-minute segment featuring Adelaide Hall who sings "Chi-Baba, Chi-Baba (My Bambino Goes to Sleep)", followed by a medley that included the song Adelaide had introduced in 1928: "I Can't Give You Anything But Love".

Before the existence of videotape, no technology existed to record television, but in the 1940s the BBC began experimenting by using a process known as telerecording. This was achieved by filming onto 35mm film stock direct from the television screen as the programme aired. The telerecording of Adelaide's performance in *Variety in Sepia* remained undiscovered in the BBC's archive until 1989 when I rediscovered it and then screened it at the National Film Theatre in April 1992, with Adelaide Hall in the audience. BBC2 then screened it on 1 July 1992. It is now recognised as the BBC's earliest known recording of a live performance by an entertainer on British television.

Sepia was transmitted live from the BBC's television studio at Alexandra Palace on 1 December 1948. Described as an "all-coloured variety show", Evelyn and Edric were featured with Mable Lee and Charles Woods. Evelyn

CASANOVA
TODAY'S SPECIAL:
Rs.
Club Sandwich each. 2/-
Fried Fish & Chips per plate. 2/-
Prawn Cutlet per plate. 1/-
Chicken Cutlet per plate. 1/-

Evelyn in India in 1949

sang "Shadrack" and the famous 1930s torch song, "Stormy Weather", long associated with black women singers including Ethel Waters (for whom it was written in 1933), Elisabeth Welch (who introduced it to British audiences in 1933), and Lena Horne (who sang it in a Hollywood movie in 1943).

As a result of their popularity on radio and television, Evelyn and Edric were partnered for a new stage musical called *Calypso* which opened at the Wimbledon Theatre on 10 May 1948. It was described in *The Stage* (13 May 1948) as:

a West Indian musical show... a mixture of musical comedy, revue, ballet, and variety. There is a very thin plot. Otherwise the show is mainly a succession of dancing scenes and songs to accompaniment of two pianos and native band. Edric Connor works hard and, of course, sings well. His best number is a negro spiritual... One of his songs, 'Democracy', is typical of calypso – a town-crier's rhyme-less ballad. Evelyn Dove's few songs are well-sung.

Most of the press attention was given to Mable Lee, a young African American jazz tap dancer, singer and entertainer who had already made an impact on Broadway and at the famed Apollo Theatre in Harlem.

1948 was something of a landmark year for black theatre in Britain. In London's West End two hugely popular American stage plays that had opened

in 1947 were still playing to packed houses: *Anna Lucasta* (His Majesty's Theatre) with an all-black cast headed by Hilda Simms and *Deep Are the Roots* (Wyndham's Theatre) starring Gordon Heath. At the Boltons Theatre the Guyanese actor Robert Adams took the lead in a production of *Native Son*, written by the African American Richard Wright and Katherine Dunham and her dance troupe, featuring a young Eartha Kitt, opened in *A Caribbean Rhapsody* at the Prince of Wales's theatre. Also in 1948, at the Globe, Elisabeth Welch was attracting attention for her starring role in a sophisticated revue called *Tuppence Coloured* in which she introduced Edith Piaf's famous song "La Vie en Rose" to Britain.

1948 was also a significant year for Britain's black community for, on 22 June that year, the *Empire Windrush* arrived with the first wave of post-war Caribbean settlers. In all, some 500 people (492 passengers and eight stowaways) landed at Tilbury. Sam King, a Jamaican who had served in the Royal Air Force in the Second World War, was among those on the ship. He later recalled in my book *Speak of me as I am – The Black Presence in Southwark Since 1600* (2005): "As we got closer to England there was great apprehension in the boat because we knew the authorities did not want us on land. So we knew we were not wanted but, being British, once we arrived at Tilbury everything humanly possible was done to help us. We from the ex-colonies have contributed a lot to the improvement of the British way of life. Nearly a third of the inner cities were destroyed by bombing—we helped to rebuild it." That same year, 1948, Evelyn received high praise from Eric Fawcett at the BBC:

I have known Miss Dove's work for the last six or seven years, from the time when I first used her in the serial *Mint Julep*, in which she took the main singing part, until her last appearance for me at Radiolympia in *Variety in Sepia*. She is a contralto with a perfect microphone quality and although I have used her mostly in music of negro origin this has ranged from spirituals and traditional airs to Coleridge-Taylor. She is, of course, a highly trained singer, and at one time intended to go into opera. Together with Edric Connor she appeared in my sound series *Serenade in Sepia*, transferring with it to television in 1946. She is an extremely charming person with a very attractive personality. I would rate her the best coloured contralto in this country.

Chapter 13: 1950s

Evelyn's radio appearance in *Breakfast Hour* on 9 January 1949 would be her last work for the BBC for almost two years. In a letter to the BBC, dated 19 December 1950, Evelyn informed the corporation that, since they had last worked together, she had made *le grand tour*, appearing in cabaret in India for eighteen months, two months in Paris and "a flying visit to Spain." Evelyn loved to travel, but now she was home again, living at an address in North London's Swiss Cottage, and eager to work. "I should like to start broadcasting again," she said. Her wish came true, and on 12 January 1951 she returned to Alexandra Palace to make a television appearance in a popular programme called *Kaleidoscope*, described in the *Radio Times* as an "entertainment magazine for the family." In the "Song Time" segment, Evelyn sang two numbers, "Cawnbread", a traditional song, and Rodgers and Hammerstein's "What's the Use of Wonderin'" from *Oklahoma*. On 25 March 1951 Evelyn returned to radio with an appearance in *Variety Bandbox*. The cast also included the comedian Arthur English and a young Peter Sellers. It was her final radio appearance.

For a while stage work interrupted her return to broadcasting. In May 1951 Evelyn joined the cast of *London Melody*, which opened at the Empress Hall, Earl's Court in West London. The cast was headed by the British born figure-skating star Belita, who had enjoyed some success in Hollywood films, and the comedian Norman Wisdom. Also featured were three black artistes, Evelyn (as Iolanthe Jones), and two former members of Katherine Dunham's dance troupe: Richardena Jackson and Ben Johnson. *The Times* (1 June 1951) described the lavish production as "A melange of musical comedy, ballet, and superb skating" and singled out Evelyn from the supporting cast, "all these things and the subtle grace of Miss Evelyn Dove go to make an admirable entertainment." Evelyn performed one song in *London Melody*, "Heart Beat" with Ben Johnson and Richardena Jackson. On 10 June 1951 BBC Television took cameras to Empress Hall and broadcast the production in their *Sunday-Night Theatre* series. It was during the run of this production that Evelyn and Richardena became close friends.

1951 was a busy year for Evelyn. Following the success of *London Melody* she joined the cast of Richard Rodgers and Oscar Hammerstein II's London version of their Broadway triumph *South Pacific*. This production opened at the Theatre Royal, Drury Lane on 1 November 1951 and starred Mary Martin from the Broadway original. Evelyn is credited in the cast as "Bloody Mary's Assistant", but it is a minor role, with no dialogue. Off-stage, Evelyn was employed as the understudy for Muriel Smith, the African American opera singer who had been cast as the Tonkinese Bloody Mary. Muriel had made her name as the original *Carmen Jones* on Broadway in 1943, Oscar Hammerstein II's adaptation of Bizet's famous opera *Carmen* with an all-black cast. After the war, Muriel moved to London and made successful appearances in West End revues before being offered *South Pacific*.

South Pacific was a big success. British critics loved it. W. A. Darlington informed readers of the *Daily Telegraph* (2 November 1951) that the musical "duly swept to its predestined triumph at Drury Lane last night. Mary Martin, too, made the greatest kind of personal success, and deserved it well. She has a strong company to back her. The music has a haunting charm." One can only speculate how Evelyn would have played Bloody Mary and taken centre stage for the character's magnificent solo, the haunting "Bali Ha'i". It is possible that she did, if Muriel had been unavailable. *South Pacific* enjoyed a long and successful run at Drury Lane for over a year before it closed on 1 January 1953.

In 1954 Evelyn joined the cast of a stage production of Alan Paton's anti-apartheid novel *Cry, the Beloved Country*. It was staged at St Martin-in-the-Fields church at the north-east corner of Trafalgar Square for three weeks from 1 February. It was adapted by Felicia Komai with the collaboration of the producer, Josephine Douglas. The cast included some of the best black British actors then working in Britain and these included the veteran Nigerian actor Orlando Martins as the Reverend Stephen Kumalo. Edric Connor was cast as the Reverend Msimangu while newcomers Lionel Ngakane (from South Africa) and Trinidad's Errol John were featured. Evelyn played two roles: Mrs Ndlela and Mrs Kumalo. *The Times* (2 February 1954) were impressed: "Mr Alan Paton's story of two men of two races are united by suffering when the native clergyman's only son is executed for the murder of the only son of a white man has been recognised as a parable for our time. The spirit of the work triumphs over any shortcomings in dramatic technique." Several of the actors, including Edric Connor and Lionel Ngakane, had recently acted in Zoltan Korda's acclaimed 1952 film version of the novel. Felicia Komai was a writer of British-Japanese heritage who was raised in London before the war surrounded by the great literary figures of the day. Her father was the Japanese poet Gmoske Komai and her godfather was the novelist H.G.

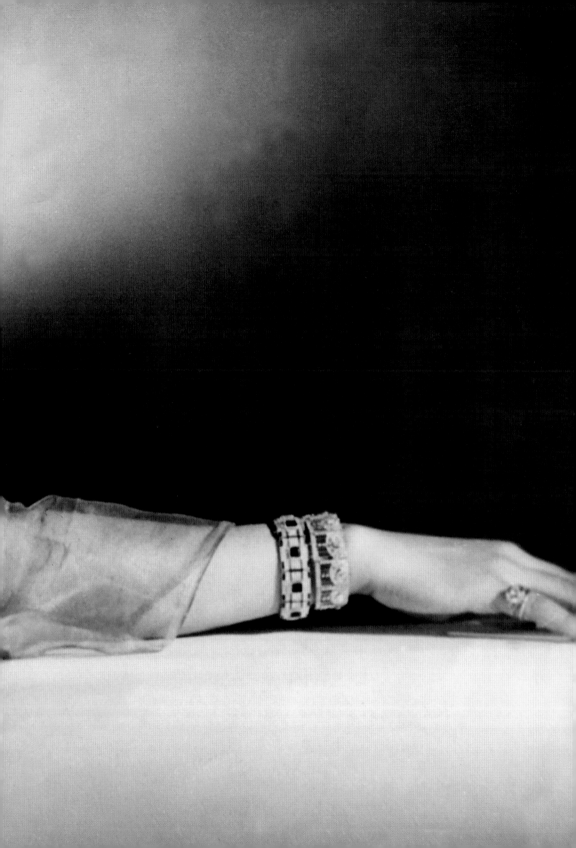

Wells. Felicia adapted Paton's novel as a verse drama. Her adaptation was later produced for British television as an ITV *Play of the Week* in 1958 with the African American Gordon Heath in the leading role of the Reverend Stephen Kumalo.

Evelyn returned to BBC Television on two occasions in 1954. The first was on 18 July in a *Sunday-Night Theatre* play by James Dyrenforth called *Halcyon Days* in which she played Mrs Carter. James Dyrenforth was a white American actor and songwriter, based in Britain, who took a leading role in the play which was set in an imaginary town in America's Deep South. The *Radio Times* described the setting of the play as Halcyon, "a little town deep in the mint julep country of Kentucky in the hot, lazy summer of 1905." In addition to Evelyn, the cast included a number of black actors then working in Britain: Gordon Heath, Nadia Cattouse, Lionel Ngakane, Pauline Henriques, Ida Shepley, Norris Smith and Connie Smith. A second live performance of *Halcyon Days* was transmitted on 22 July. According to the BBC's Audience Research Report, viewers enjoyed *Halcyon Days*: "A number of viewers who evidently have 'a soft spot' for stories about the Deep South enjoyed this play very much... According to one group, the plot was agreeably innocuous yet had sufficient 'grip' in its concern with human relationships and the problems of the colour bar to hold attention

throughout... The acting was thought very good with James Dyrenforth (Judge Lowrey), Gordon Heath and Sylvia Overman outstanding." On 2 August Evelyn appeared in *Music for You*. Eric Robinson conducted the orchestra and Evelyn sang "Ma Curly Headed Baby", a song once popularised by Paul Robeson who sang it in one of his British films *Big Fella* (1937). On 5 January 1955 Evelyn made her final television appearance as a singer in *Meet the Commonwealth* in which she sang the spiritual "Don't Ask Me Lawd".

Before the end of 1955, singing and acting work had become so scarce that Evelyn applied for a job as a telephonist. The BBC was contacted in September 1955 for a reference. It is not known if the BBC gave Evelyn a reference, but it is likely that she must have been forced, from time to time, to seek work outside the world of entertainment. Evelyn had to survive. Some months later the BBC offered her a featured role as Eartha Kitt's mother in a *Sunday-Night Theatre* presentation of the Broadway play *Mrs Patterson* (see Chapter 14).

In 1957 Evelyn played obligatory "maid" roles in two productions. For television, this time ITV (16 January), she played Coralee in a *Play of the Week* production of Lillian Hellman's *Another Part of the Forest*. This was Hellman's prequel to her earlier play *The Little Foxes* and had originally been produced on Broadway in 1946. Later that year Evelyn was cast in a minor role in the

Orlando Martins, Evelyn and unidentified actor
in *Cry, the Beloved Country* (1954)

British film melodrama *The Story of Esther Costello*, starring the Hollywood legend Joan Crawford. Newcomer Heather Sears won a BAFTA for her critically acclaimed portrayal of a deaf, dumb and blind girl who is adopted by Crawford. Evelyn has an almost silent role as Joan Crawford's maid Sue and was not credited on the cast list. In 1957 *The Story of Esther Costello* was a popular success in Britain. That year it was listed 11th among the top money-making films at the British box office.

The acclaimed African American poet and playwright Langston Hughes adapted *Simply Heavenly*, described as "A Comedy with Music", from his novel *Simple Takes a Wife*. It featured an all-black cast and stood out from other black American shows in that Hughes's characters retained their culture instead of avoiding it. Until then, black musical characters created by whites tended to lose their culture and heritage unless they lived on a Caribbean island. Hughes also wrote the lyrics, while David Martin contributed the music. Says Allen Woll in *Black Musical Theatre* (1989): "Hughes worked virtually alone for the next several years to revive the black musical for the age of the civil rights movement."

Simply Heavenly played on Broadway in 1957 before crossing the Atlantic for its European premiere at the Manchester Palace on 15 April 1958. The British production opened in London's West End at the Adelphi Theatre on 20 May 1958. It was directed by the celebrated actor Laurence Harvey who persuaded the producer Jack Hylton to allow him to try his hand at directing with this new production. An attractive cast was headed by the extrovert singer and actress Bertice Reading and two members of the American cast: Melvin Stewart and John Bouie. The rest of the cast included Evelyn (as Mrs Caddy), her friends Richardena Jackson and Isabelle Lucas, and many British or European-based black artistes such as Earl Cameron, Marpessa Dawn (soon to become a star in the film *Black Orpheus*), Bari Johnson, Ilene Day and Harry Baird. Reviews were, on the whole, disappointing though *The Times* (21 May 1958) described it as a "pleasant entertainment" and acknowledged that Bertice Reading "did wonders throughout" as Miss Mamie.

After *Simply Heavenly* closed, Evelyn joined another all-black cast but in doing so she found herself caught up in a frightening situation during the summer of 1958. She accepted the role of Noah's Wife in a BBC Television version of Marc Connelly's *The Green Pastures*. This American play, which re-enacted scenes from the Bible using black actors, was first staged on Broadway in 1930 and filmed in Hollywood in 1936. The BBC broadcast two radio versions, in 1945 and 1956, before presenting it as a *Sunday-Night Theatre* production on 14 September 1958. The BBC cast around sixty black actors based in Britain, including Evelyn, her friend Richardena Jackson and Nadia Cattouse, who played the schoolteacher, Mrs Deshee. But the leading role was given to an American, William Marshall, who was brought over to play the lead, and his casting in the play caused a great deal of upset among the British black actors in the cast.

Most of the actors in *The Green Pastures*, including Evelyn, were on the books of the Edric Connor Agency. In 1956 Edric and his wife Pearl had founded the agency to represent artists, writers, and actors who had come to Britain in the post-war years from Africa, Malaysia, India and the Caribbean. When I interviewed Pearl in 1993, she told me:

Edric and I decided to do something for them, and we became the first agency to represent them. Also they kept inviting black stars and actors over from America, like Harry Belafonte, Eartha Kitt and William Marshall. Edric was very upset when the BBC didn't cast him in the television version of *The Green Pastures*. They gave the lead to William Marshall. The American blacks had glamour and celebrity status which gave them the edge on Britain's black performers. We had no media attention. No press coverage. In Britain our actors had to make it on pure merit and friends. We even fought with Equity to give more chances to British black actors because they kept bringing over Americans. We had a very difficult time convincing casting directors that our black actors could act.

The Green Pastures was produced by Eric Fawcett, who had employed Evelyn many times in the 1940s on radio and television, including the popular series *Serenade in Sepia*, and Fawcett also planned to cast Edric Connor in the leading role of "De Lawd (The Lord)", but hit the obstacle mentioned by Pearl Connor. Edric later explained what happened in his autobiography *Horizons*:

In February 1958 I had been asked by Eric Fawcett to give a confidential report on all the Negro actors in Britain. He was expecting to produce *Green Pastures* later in the year, and wanted me to play De Lawd. He was given the all clear. He telephoned, asking me to attend at the BBC on 10 August (1958) to meet Marc Connelly, the author of *Green Pastures*. I duly attended, and Marc Connelly made me read the whole of De Lawd in his play. He couldn't find any flaws. I discovered he was forcing himself to find flaws in my performance. After an hour I took up my photographs and newspaper cuttings and left. Cordially. A few days later I discovered that Marc Connolly brought a man with him from the United States and had installed him in London. No matter how well I may have read, he had brought his friend to play De Lawd. I had already played the role on stage and on sound radio.

CRY, THE BELOVED COUNTRY

A verse-drama by
FELICIA KOMAI from the
novel by ALAN PATON

News got around that I was good enough for the Shakespeare Memorial Theatre, but somehow not for Connolly. The Negro artistes, while accepting the jobs, insisted they were not going to work with this American, who had been brought in through the back door. Connolly began to play tough. He said if I couldn't get the artistes he wanted in his play, there wasn't going to be no play. While I felt flattered at the action taken by the British Negro actors, I realised that it was not often sixty of them could get work at one and the same time. I chased them all to work—told them to go and show their real ability.

The casting of an African American in a British production was nothing new. There has always been a tradition in Britain of overlooking black British actors and casting visiting African Americans instead. Famous examples include four important films of the 1960s: John Kitzmiller in *Dr No* (1962), Brock Peters in *The L-Shaped Room* (1962), Ossie Davis in *The Hill* (1965) and Sidney Poitier in *To Sir, With Love* (1967). Fine actors, but their British counterparts, actors like Edric, Earl Cameron, Errol John, Calvin Lockhart and Johnny Sekka, were denied these roles and their careers suffered as a result. However, in his autobiography, the aggrieved Edric had the last word on William Marshall: "De Lawd was so insecure His angels walked all over Him."

When I interviewed Nadia Cattouse in 1989, she remembered that the rehearsals for *The Green Pastures* took place in Notting Hill at the time of the anti-black "race" riots:

I remember that day in 1958 when we were rehearsing *The Green Pastures* in a schoolroom in Notting Hill. The riots had started. One afternoon we noticed a gathering of about a dozen white youths, "Teddy" boys, outside on the street looking very threateningly towards the building, and then the numbers started to grow. The BBC was informed about this and they were concerned for our safety. They believed we were in danger. Decisions were quickly made and a bus arrived to get us out. The entire cast was asked to get on it, whether we lived in Notting Hill or not. However, one of the senior members of the cast, an elderly actor called Rudy Evans, refused to get on the bus. He told the man from the BBC that he lived nearby and was going to walk home. If any white "Teddy" boys tried to attack him, he would deal with them! I shall never forget that fearless old man. He was from the generation who had been here from before the war. He said something like "I walk in the cloak of righteousness. They will not harm me." And the man from the BBC said, "yes, I understand, but please get on the bus." But Rudy refused. The bus took the rest of us to Hammersmith tube station and we had to make our own way home from there. The next day the BBC found us an alternative rehearsal room in Ealing.

Britain's African Caribbean population continued to grow throughout the fifties, and in West End theatre, 1958 was a watershed year for black productions and must have kept the Edric Connor Agency very busy. In addition to *Simply Heavenly*, there was *Moon on a Rainbow Shawl* at the Royal Court, written by the Trinidadian actor Errol John. The Jamaican dramatist Barry Reckord had his play *Flesh to a Tiger* produced at the Royal Court. It starred the jazz singer Cleo Laine in her first dramatic role. Shelagh Delaney's acclaimed *A Taste of Honey* was premiered at the Theatre Royal, Stratford with Jimmie Moore as the black sailor and Ted Willis's *Hot Summer Night* confronted racism in 1950s Britain at the New Theatre with the Jamaican actor Lloyd Reckord in the lead. Outside London Edric Connor became the first black actor to appear with the Royal Shakespeare Company at Stratford-upon-Avon when he played Gower in Shakespeare's *Pericles*.

It seemed the times were changing, but Evelyn faced a problem when it came to being cast. Directors avoided casting her as a middle-class Englishwoman, a role she was born to play. Instead she played either Africans (*Cry, the Beloved Country*) or African Americans (*Halcyon Days, Mrs Patterson, Simply Heavenly, The Green Pastures*) which she did convincingly. There was nothing wrong with that, but such roles for an older actress were scarce.

Chapter 14: Eartha Kitt and Mrs Patterson

On British television in the 1950s, leading dramatic roles for black actresses were almost non-existent, and the few that were available were usually offered to visiting American celebrities. But, in some instances, they provided supporting roles for British based black artistes, like Evelyn Dove. In 1956 the American singer Eartha Kitt visited Britain for a cabaret season at London's top nightspot, the Café de Paris. During this visit Eartha accepted an offer to play a mysterious convicted murderess on death row in a BBC Television drama called *The Valiant*. It was transmitted live on 15 May 1956, but no recording exists. With this appearance, Eartha was given a high profile by the BBC and she became the first black woman to be featured on the cover of their popular listings magazine *Radio Times*. One month later Eartha returned to BBC Television to play another major dramatic role in *Mrs Patterson*, an adaptation of her 1954 Broadway stage success.

Mrs Patterson was showcased by the BBC on 17 June 1956 in their popular *Sunday-Night Theatre* slot. This was the BBC's inaugural production from their new Riverside Studios in Hammersmith which may explain why it was telerecorded and therefore saved for posterity. In addition to Eartha, the production offered roles to several British based black artistes including Elisabeth Welch as the blues singer Bessie Bolt and Evelyn, who made a rare appearance in a non-singing acting role as Eartha's mother, Anna Hicks.

Set in the 1920s, *Mrs Patterson* tells the story of Theodora 'Teddy' Hicks, a fifteen-year-old poverty stricken black girl from the rural Kentucky in the American South. She lives in a fantasy world in which she dreams of being a rich white lady like her mother's snobbish employer, Mrs Patterson. The play had been written by Charles Sebree and Greer Johnson for Eartha and presented on the New York stage at the National Theatre in 1954. It was one of the first Broadway productions during the 1950s to be written by an African American. Sebree, who co-authored with the white Johnson, was a black gay man who had been a dancer, painter, and scene designer with the American Negro Theatre. *Mrs Patterson* was adapted from his earlier non-musical fantasy *My Mother Came Crying Most Pitifully* (1949). Eartha's co-star, Terry Carter, interviewed by John L. Williams for his biography *America's Mistress*

– *The Life and Times of Eartha Kitt* (2013), remembered Sebree as "a very pleasant fellow, smooth and funny" and that the play was a vehicle for Eartha: "It was quite evident to me that she was in command of everything around her. She acted like the star she was—even though she hadn't been one for very long—she was very self-assertive. She had a good sense of humour, but you had to be on the good side of her. Eartha was very determined to make it work. I think she did a great job."

Eartha Kitt's rise to fame had been meteoric. After starting out as a dancer with Katherine Dunham's dance troupe, she had earned a modest reputation in Paris as a cabaret singer before being triumphantly showcased in the Broadway revue *New Faces of 1952*. Eartha readily agreed to star in *Mrs Patterson* because it offered her an opportunity to extend her range as a dramatic actress. However, to accommodate Eartha's fame as a singer, the authors interpolated five songs during Teddy's "dream" sequences.

Although most theatre critics were disappointed by the play, many praised Eartha's performance in a demanding and difficult role. Miles Jefferson applauded Eartha in his review in the journal *Phylon*: "Her scintillating gamine personality threw light in many a dark corner of the play." Brooks Atkinson, the esteemed theatre critic who worked for *The New York Times*, described Eartha as "an incandescent young woman with lively intelligence, a darting sense of movement, keen eyes and an instinct for the stage." Only George Jean Nathan, critic for the New York *Journal American*, was critical. Hostile to black productions and actors, he described Eartha as a "Negro topsy" who "made something of a hit, for no discernible reason other than she was colored."

For Eartha, *Mrs Patterson* was the breakthrough she had been seeking. It launched her into an even more successful career as a singer who could act. She later recalled in her autobiography *I'm Still Here* (1989): "*Mrs Patterson* opened in New York to great critical acclaim for Eartha Kitt. When I went to the theatre the morning after the opening, the front of house on 41st Street was covered with blow-ups of the reviews; I was hailed as one of the greatest artists of our time... To be acclaimed now as a great actress was really a coup, particularly as my character had to sustain a whole evening."

In 1989 I interviewed Eartha Kitt for the magazine *Films and Filming*. The interview took place in her dressing room at the Shaftesbury Theatre in London. At the time she was appearing in Stephen Sondheim's musical *Follies*. It had taken several months to find me a "slot" and I was nervous at meeting her. I had been informed by her personal assistant that Eartha expected me to purchase a plant for the star. That didn't help my fear of meeting her. On entering her dressing room and coming face to face with Miss Kitt, I couldn't help but notice numerous plants around the room, and two white doves roosting in a birdcage on a shelf. I felt intimidated. Miss Kitt had a reputation for being formidable but as soon as she realised I was not there to fire questions at her about her private life and pry into her love life, she became relaxed and was extremely kind and generous towards me.

When I asked Eartha about her film and television career, we discussed the BBC Television version of *Mrs Patterson*:

I was drawn to the story because of its setting, the rural American south, where I was raised. So I knew about that place. And when I was a kid I was a dreamer. *Mrs Patterson* is about a young girl who has very strong dreams and desires of living a life the way white people live. The songs were written because I was known as a singer. The television version had to be produced in Britain because American television wouldn't touch a mixed black and white cast at that time. They were afraid of the subject even though the mixed cast in that situation didn't have anything to do with love or whatever. There was no love affair between the races depicted in *Mrs Patterson*. I enjoyed doing the television version very much. We had a marvellous cast and I enjoyed working with Elisabeth Welch, who was very well-known in Britain, and Evelyn Dove, who played my mother. The scenery was absolutely beautiful. The artificial magnolia trees were almost as alive as the actual thing. I was very fascinated by the fact that there was

such artistry in the scenery and I liked that group of people, not just the cast, but the crew as well. Everything was so professional, the stagehands, the lighting, the sets were very beautiful.

In the *Radio Times* (15 June 1956) Peter Currie described *Mrs Patterson* as an:

unusual and touching comedy of adolescence. [Eartha is] an artist of considerable range, surely indicated by her recent television appearance in *The Valiant*: the brooding, withdrawn murderess in that play could hardly have been further removed from the celebrated, sardonic, mischief-eyed Delilah of cabaret and records. In her second appearance in this country as a straight actress, she gives additional proof of her versatility by playing the part of a teenage girl who dreams of escaping from her boredom at home.

When Ivor Brown reviewed *Mrs Patterson* in the popular BBC journal *The Listener* (21 June 1956), he was particularly impressed with the "strong, unsentimental urgency" of Eartha Kitt's performance. *The Times* (18 June 1956) acknowledged that "Sebree and Johnson have written a part that does not diminish Miss Eartha Kitt... The cast was strong, and the silhouette background for the daydream episodes was wanly evocative."

Overall, the reviews for *Mrs Patterson* and Eartha Kitt's performance were favourable. By sharp contrast, the 221 viewers who completed a questionnaire for the BBC's Audience Research Report, compiled by the Audience Research Department, were mostly negative. Based on their responses to different parts of the production, the BBC rated *Mrs Patterson* with a "Reaction Index" of 44, which was very far below the average of 68 for studio plays transmitted at this time: "The commonest feeling was that good acting (and singing) had been wasted on poor material". A very small minority of viewers "found the play itself charming and were moved by the story." Eartha's performance was enjoyed, and "of the rest of the cast, Evelyn Dove (Anna Hicks) was most frequently mentioned by name."

I first saw the telerecording of *Mrs Patterson* at a private screening with Elisabeth 'Lis' Welch at the British Film Institute (BFI) in 1988. Lis and I shared a mutual friend, an employee at the BFI, and he happily arranged for their archive recording of *Mrs Patterson* to be screened for us. Lis enjoyed the screening, and laughed out loud at the set: "it looks more like the arctic than the Deep South!" She was puzzled by her character, Bessie Bolt, who sat in a tree while conversing with Eartha down below. Perhaps Lis did not fully appreciate that her scenes were part of a fantasy world, conjured up by Eartha's character. Afterwards, Lis and I engaged in conversation about the play. The screening brought back many

memories for her. Sadly, Eartha Kitt did not make a good impression on her. Lis found her aloof and unfriendly during rehearsals, but acknowledged that the young actress had a demanding role to enact and sustain in front of the television cameras. Lis remembered working with Evelyn at the beginning of the war in a popular BBC Radio series called *Rhapsody in Black* and she was impressed with Evelyn's fine performance as Eartha's hard-working mother in *Mrs Patterson*. Lis acknowledged that, though well-known as a singer, Evelyn had been underrated as a "straight" actress, and should have done more dramatic work.

In 1994 I included *Mrs Patterson* in a National Film Theatre film and television retrospective dedicated to Elisabeth Welch's screen career, but the recording of the play remained unseen in the National Film and Television Archive for over twenty years until revived again, at the National Film Theatre, in 2015. It was included in the *Classics on TV: Great American Playwrights* season and the screening was presented by Dr Amanda Wrigley, a Research Fellow at the University of Westminster. In her programme note, handed out to the audience at the screening, she acknowledged that Eartha is "captivating" as Teddy Hicks:

who spends much of her time daydreaming about living the life of luxury she imagines is enjoyed by her

mother's wealthy and well-travelled white employer, the "Mrs Patterson" of the play's title. Songs from Kitt and Elisabeth Welch characterise the sequences arising from Teddy's rich imagination, giving the performance a rich fantastical dimension which permits her to play cards with the Devil and to be included in Mrs Patterson's sophisticated social gatherings. The reality of her life breaks in increasingly, however, and a crisis point is reached when she agrees to run off to Chicago with Willie B., the boy-next-door played by Neville Crabbe. Evelyn Dove plays Teddy's mother with grace and poise and Estelle Winwood is the Mrs Patterson of Teddy's fantasies.

Eartha's career was given a boost by *Mrs Patterson*. It established her as a singer who could also act, and her versatility led to several more dramatic roles in films, including *Anna Lucasta* (1958), and on television. However, her career in America took a downward slide when, in 1968 she was invited to a White House luncheon given by President Lyndon Johnson's wife, Lady Bird Johnson. As it turned out, it was an invitation to disaster. In the course of a conversation with Lady Bird Johnson, Eartha spoke out against the Vietnam War and her candidness quickly resulted in FBI and CIA investigations of both her professional and personal life. Her career suffered for years after her White House visit. A decade later Eartha made a spectacular comeback as the star of the hit Broadway musical *Timbuktu!* (1978), a black-cast version of *Kismet* which earned her a Tony nomination. It demonstrated that the FBI and CIA could not keep her away from her adoring fans. Eartha was a fighter and a survivor who continued to surprise and delight her audiences with each new venture, whether it be a camp gay disco pop record, a one-woman show, a television appearance or a role in a film. Until she passed away on Christmas Day 2008, unpredictable Eartha was, as Sidney Poitier once described her, "one of a kind."

Chapter 15: Negro Theatre Workshop

Edric and Pearl Connor were ambitious. In addition to their agency, they dreamed of running a black British theatre company. Not only would it provide work for actors on their agency's books, but they believed that such a venture would help promote the work of African and Caribbean playwrights. In 1961 they launched the Negro Theatre Workshop (NTW), but from the start the Connors faced problems attracting financial support and securing a base. While initially at the office of their theatrical agency: 6 Paddington Street in London, when the Africa Centre was opened in its spacious premises in Covent Garden (informally 1962, officially 1964), the Workshop used it for rehearsal and performance of some of its productions. Pearl Connor told me:

The Negro Theatre Workshop came about because we had very little work coming in, and we decided to try and put together things that we could present ourselves and invite people to come and see. The Africa Centre in London had just been established and they had an empty hall which we were able to use very cheaply. So we gathered our people together and, after *A Wreath for Udomo* in 1961, the first really major thing we tried to do was a

blues version of the St Luke Passion called, if you please, *The Dark Disciples*!

Before the 1960s there had been several attempts to establish black theatre companies in Britain. For example, in 1944 the film and stage actor Robert Adams founded the Negro Repertory Theatre. With himself playing the lead, he presented Eugene O'Neill's *All God's Chillun' Got Wings* with the Colchester Repertory Company. However, Adams was ahead of his time and the group did not survive. In 1947 and 1948 Pauline Henriques and several other black British actors were employed as the understudies of the African American cast of *Anna Lucasta*, a successful play that had transferred from New York to London's West End for a long run at His Majesty's Theatre. With little to do backstage, in pursuit of her craft Pauline organised the other understudies into the Negro Theatre Company. In 1948 they staged an evening of poetry and drama which they called *Something Different*. Pauline later described the Company as the "nucleus of what we were beginning to think of as the British Black Theatre Movement."

In 1961 Edric and Pearl Connor staged their first production, *A Wreath for*

Udomo. A few days before the 1 November preview, *The Times* (27 October 1961) noted that this performance would be given to help raise money for the NTW and the West Indian Theatre Trust (co-founded by Pearl to support the NTW): "The purpose is to help West Indian actors, playwrights, producers and designers to begin or to continue working in London theatre."

The play opened at the Lyric, Hammersmith on 2 November with NTW member Evelyn in the supporting cast. It was directed by Philip Burton, the Welshman who had taught and then adopted the actor Richard Burton. *A Wreath for Udomo* was adapted by the African American playwright William Branch from a South African novel by the black writer Peter Abrahams. The theme of the play is the birth of an African nation and the corruption of the young revolutionary who becomes its first Prime Minister. The cast also included Edric Connor, Earl Cameron, Lloyd Reckord, Andre Dakar, Joan Hooley, Harry Baird and Horace James. The 1 November preview included a steel

Lloyd Reckord, Earl Cameron and Evelyn in *A Wreath for Udomo* (1961)

Evelyn (centre) in *The Dark Disciples* (1965)

band and a Creole supper prepared by Pearl, but disaster struck on the official opening night. As noted in *The Times* (3 November 1961), during the second act, Edric Connor collapsed during a scene in which he was holding the centre of the stage: "The other players went to his assistance, but Mr Connor could not continue. The curtain was lowered." Connor had suffered a heart attack and had to be replaced by Leo Carera. Six days later, on 8 November, *A Wreath for Udomo* reopened. On the whole, the reviews were favourable. *The Times* (9 November 1961) felt that "The second half proved to be far more interesting than the first" and singled out Earl Cameron for praise for his "unforced treatment of the last scenes." Evelyn was positively mentioned in several reviews. Eric Shorter in the *Daily Telegraph* (9 November 1961) acknowledged that "Lloyd Reckord, Evelyn Dove, John Arnatt and Leo Carera take their chances well" while Denis Hart in *The Guardian* (9 November 1961) described the cast as excellent and praised Evelyn for her portrayal of Selina, "the wise and powerful tribal woman." Sadly, *Udomo* closed after a brief two-week run.

Evelyn's next professional engagement was as the Narrator in the NTW's production of *The Dark Disciples*. It was described in *The Stage* (22 April 1965) as "The blues version of the St Luke Passion presented by the Negro Theatre Workshop as *The Dark Disciples*" and finished its tour of churches in the

London area on Good Friday, 1965. *The Stage* continued:

Earlier this week they gave three performances at St. Martin-in-the-Fields, a church whose theatrical association makes it an appropriate setting for a dramatised account of the Easter story. Christian Simpson's production made use of singers, actors and dancers, blending their diverse talents in a piece of teamwork marked by singular devotion to the task of recreating the great story in contemporary terms. With the crowd playing the largest part in the action, the principal characters, particularly Christ, seem diminished in size and the actual crucifixion occurs as just another incident, thus weakening the overall impact of the story. A small instrumental group, consisting of piano, double-bass and percussion, provided the musical accompaniment, which Mike McKenzie had arranged as an uncomplicated expression of the spirit of the Passion. Some of the music is moving in this context, and the chorus work gives several opportunities for lively singing as well as the quieter style of the chorales. Even the soloists' recitatives are written in a rhythmic blues manner, and there is one especially fine solo for a boy soprano, sung with great feeling by an unidentified boy. Dancing plays a relatively unimportant part in the play, except to add movement to the crowd scenes, and it was not used to heighten the effect of the situation as often as it might have been. A solid-looking table was the only prop, and this served

for the Last Supper and later unfolded to become the cross. Lighting conditions were difficult, but one moment of true theatre came when a solitary glow from below and behind the cross outlined the figure of the dead Christ, while smoke floated slowly upward.

It is not known if Evelyn travelled with the NTW to Senegal in 1966. In an interview I had with Pearl she explained that:

It was Easter 1966 and there was a World Festival of Black and African Arts happening in Senegal. We took *The Dark Disciples* there and performed it very successfully in the big Dakar Cathedral. We also took a play by the Nigerian playwright, Obi Egbuna, called *Wind versus Polygamy*. Earl Cameron was among the very distinguished artistes who went out to perform in that play. We made an enormous impact in Senegal, and that helped us to establish some of the people in the group professionally.

On returning to Britain Pearl, representing the black actors on her agency's books, took her case to Equity. She said:

We could not live in a vacuum, we had to work something out regarding the forty weeks eligibility rule, and that the criteria set up for British artistes could not possibly be suitable for us. Of course, their answer was that there was no difference, that they did not accept that there was a difference between people. We couldn't agree, and it has subsequently been acknowledged... But, in those days, people didn't want to see that there was a difference, that black artistes were being ignored, were not known about. And because it was impossible to become known, we couldn't get Equity membership.

Evelyn made her final professional appearance in *The Dark Disciples*, acting with one of Britain's first black theatre companies. Her professional career had brought her a long way from 1920s revues like *The Chocolate Kiddies* and *Brownbirds*. However, her stage career had come full circle. It had begun with the all-black cast revues of the 1920s and it would end with an all-black cast dramatisation of the St Luke Passion. Evelyn was in her sixties now, and looking tired. Among her possessions was a copy of the script for *The Dark Disciples*. The last surviving photograph of Evelyn shows her as the Narrator in a scene from *The Dark Disciples* in 1965, surrounded by a group of black actresses. Her face tells a million stories, of triumphs, heartbreaks, excitement and disappointments.

The final memo in her BBC Personality File held at the BBC's Written Archives is brief, but it tells us a great deal about Evelyn's decline. At the age of sixty, in 1962, she wrote to the BBC and informed them about her most recent appearances, including *A Wreath for Udomo*. However, Evelyn never worked for the BBC again after her appearance in the television play *The Green Pastures* in 1958. Evelyn was at the end of her professional career and at the end of the road.

Evelyn's devoted friend
Isabelle Lucas

for Evelyn with love
Isabelle

Chapter 16: Spirit of a Dove

In 1954 Isabelle Lucas travelled to Britain from her birthplace in Canada, hoping for a career on the concert platform. She told me, "I loved opera and when I came to live in London it was my ambition to see concerts at the Albert Hall and Adelaide Hall. Until I arrived here, I had no idea that Adelaide Hall was a person, not a concert hall! I studied opera but Covent Garden and Sadler's Wells turned me away. There were no openings for black opera singers in Britain at that time." Penniless and desperate for work, in 1955 she saw an advertisement in *The Stage* newspaper and successfully auditioned for *The Jazz Train*, a revue at the Piccadilly Theatre: "I sang 'Dat's Love' from *Carmen Jones* so my ambition to sing opera on the London stage was fulfilled, but not at Covent Garden!" After *The Jazz Train* Isabelle successfully combined a singing and acting career with many stage and television appearances, but she remembered the 1950s "scramble for work" for Britain's black actresses and the competition they faced from well-known African Americans: "They had the edge on us because, as far as casting directors and producers were concerned, they had more experience than us, as well as glamour. I didn't think this was

fair. But in the 1950s and 1960s, if there was a part for a black woman in a play, with very few exceptions she was usually a maid or part of a race problem drama."

Isabelle's stage work over the next few decades combined musicals with serious drama and these included *Ex-Africa* at the 1963 Edinburgh Festival, described as "a black odyssey in jazz, rhyme and calypso"; Bertolt Brecht's *The Caucasian Chalk Circle* (1964), a Glasgow Citizens' production in which she was the first woman to play the Storyteller; the Negro Theatre Workshop's *Bethlehem Blues* (1964); and as Barbra Streisand's maid in the 1966 London production of the hit Broadway musical *Funny Girl*. In 1968, in an inspired piece of casting, she and Thomas Baptiste were cast as the first black Martha and George in Edward Albee's *Who's Afraid of Virginia Woolf* in a production at the Connaught Theatre in Worthing. She then joined the National Theatre at the Old Vic in 1969 to appear in George Bernard Shaw's *Back to Methuselah* and Peter Nichols's *The National Health*. Her association with Britain's black theatre movement included Mustapha Matura's *Trinidad Sisters* (1988), a black-cast version of Chekhov's *Three Sisters* for the Tricycle Theatre Company at the Donmar Warehouse. Isabelle's best-known television role was Lenny Henry's mother in Britain's first black-cast sitcom, *The Fosters*, for London Weekend Television (1976–77). In 1991 she was reunited with Norman Beaton and Carmen Munroe, her co-stars in *The Fosters*, in an episode of the popular Channel 4 sitcom *Desmond's*. In 1993 she worked throughout the summer at Regent's Park Open Air Theatre playing the Nurse in *Romeo and Juliet*, directed by Judi Dench, "a marvellous experience," she told me in a letter dated 15 September 1993.

Isabelle remembered meeting Evelyn for the first time in 1955 during the run of the West End musical *The Jazz Train*:

I was in the cast with Richardena Jackson and Evelyn was Richardena's friend. They had worked together in a show called *London Melody* in 1951. When I first met Evelyn she wore the most beautiful saris and at first I thought she was Indian. She told me she had spent some time doing cabaret in India. Then the three of us were in the cast of the musical *Simply Heavenly* in 1958. I was also the understudy for Bertice Reading, who was the star of the show. I liked Evelyn. She was beautiful but she had one or two failings. She was reckless with money and liked to glamorise

Evelyn, the cabaret queen (Italy, 1930s)

things. It was around that time that Evelyn raised a few eyebrows when she married a much younger man called Willie Brantley. He was an American black, serving in the American Air Force. Evelyn was in her fifties, and he was in his twenties.

According to their marriage certificate, Evelyn married Willie Newton Brantley on 6 September 1958 at the Register Office in St Pancras. She was 56 and he was 27. His occupation was described on the certificate as an "Airman, 1st Class, 3053102, United States Air Force". Evelyn entered her profession as "Stage Artiste". Willie was based at the Royal Air Force Station in Greenham Common, Buckinghamshire. Evelyn gave her address as 2 Conway Street, St Pancras. Isabelle recalled: "I heard that she married him because she wanted to get to America, but the American Air Force wouldn't give her permission to go there, and the marriage ended. Willie was packed off back to America without her. I think this may have been the start of her decline." Further investigation revealed that Staff Sergeant Willie Newton Brantley, born 2 September 1931, died in Dade, Florida on 14 May 1980 at the age of forty-eight.

When Evelyn married Willie in 1958, she had lost her mother and brother Frank. It is unclear if she truly loved Willie, or was just using him to get to America. On the marriage certificate she entered her name as "Evelyn *Augusta*", honouring the memory of her beloved mother by substituting her name Augusta for her true middle name, Mary.

Isabelle remembered that the 1960s was a difficult time for Evelyn. Her marriage to Willie Brantley was over, and work became scarce: "The situation with Willie ruined her emotionally and she struggled financially. Eventually the money ran out. For years her father's solicitor supported her, sometimes out of his own pocket. It became a desperate situation."

In 1972, suffering from depression, Evelyn entered Horton Hospital, a nursing home in Epsom, Surrey. Her sister-in-law, Mrs Amelia Dove, was named as her next-of-kin, but when Amelia passed away in 1976 contact with the Dove family appears to have ended. Evelyn remained at Horton Hospital for fourteen years and Isabelle stayed loyal to her friend right to the end, visiting her, and sending her letters and postcards: "I felt very sorry for her, because she had so much beauty and talent, so much to give. I stayed in touch with Evelyn until she died. She was still a lovely woman when she was old. I went to her funeral, but no one else did. Just one or two members of staff from the nursing home. It made me feel very sad."

Evelyn Dove died on 7 March 1987. She was ahead of her time, forging new barriers and facing up to her own personal struggles with determination and defiance. In the end these struggles may have defeated her, but her spirit remains alive.

Postscript

In 1942 Evelyn's portrait was painted by Louis Ginnett (1875–1946), a well-known painter of portraits and interiors, a mural painter and a designer of stained glass. He exhibited widely in his lifetime, including at the Royal Academy, and he was one of the British artists selected to be exhibited by the British Council in 1912 in Venice. Ginnett was a member of the Brighton Arts Club and lived at Nye Bungalow, Ditchling in East Sussex, not far from The Manor House in Hurstpierpoint, the home of Evelyn's mother and step-father in the 1930s and 1940s. When Evelyn passed away in 1987, her friend Isabelle Lucas inherited the portrait, and displayed it in her home in Kingston upon Thames. Isabelle and her husband Maurice Jennings kindly allowed me to photograph Evelyn's portrait.

In 1995 Isabelle Lucas suffered a heart attack and, while recovering at home, she wrote to me on 7 June that year and asked if she could pass all the Evelyn Dove memorabilia to me. I immediately called her to say "yes" and Isabelle sounded relieved. "I want you to have it," she said, "because I know you will take good care of everything. I hate the idea of everything being thrown away." Not long afterwards I collected the small trunk from Isabelle which contained Evelyn Dove's treasures. On 24 February 1997, Isabelle passed away but I do not know what happened to Louis Ginnett's portrait of Evelyn. I continued researching Evelyn's life and career, adding more and more information to the story and finding ways of sharing it with the public.

In 2004 I contributed a short biography of Evelyn to the *Oxford Dictionary of National Biography*. In 2007 I loaned a photograph of Evelyn to Sonia Boyce, a British artist of African Caribbean descent, for her *Devotional* installation at the National Portrait Gallery. Sonia's beautiful hand-drawn installation on gallery walls was a veritable roll call of some one hundred and eighty black women in British music. In addition to the installation, the image of Evelyn that I loaned to Sonia was included among the photographic portraits also displayed. Adelaide Hall, Winifred Atwell, Cleo Laine, Shirley Bassey, Millie Small, Linda Lewis, Joan Armatrading, Poly Styrene, Janet Kay, Neneh Cherry, Sade, Mica Paris and Ms. Dynamite were among some of the others whose images were included.

In 2014 I was contacted by a lady called Moira with an offer I couldn't

Evelyn's portrait, by Louis Ginnett (1942), courtesy of Christopher Ginnett

refuse. She had been researching Evelyn Dove on the internet, but had found very little information about her, except my contribution to the *Oxford Dictionary of National Biography*, which had been made available to read online. Moira was in the process of moving house and had found some possessions that had belonged to a member of her family who had passed away. The possessions included Evelyn's Bronze and Silver medals from the Royal Academy of Music. Evelyn's name was engraved on them, so Moira was able to identify her. The deceased family member had been a former employee at Horton Hospital, Evelyn's place of residence from 1972 to 1987. When the hospital was in the process of closing down, she had found the medals at the back of a cupboard and taken them home. Moira offered them to me, at no cost. I accepted but felt strongly that it was meant to be. I had often wondered what had become of Evelyn's Royal Academy of Music medals.

In 2015 I offered to the National Portrait Gallery, from my own private collection, several original photos of black British artistes for their collection. Subsequently they purchased photographic portraits of Edric Connor, Errol John and Evelyn Dove and I used the payment to help digitally restore some of Evelyn's photographs.

Appendix A: Brighton and Hove Connections

Historically, Britain's black communities have been associated with the working class dockland areas of seaports like Cardiff, Liverpool and London's East End. And yet research has shown that British citizens of African descent, or black visitors to this country, can be found in all walks of life, in many parts of the country. For many years, Evelyn and her family were connected to the East Sussex seaside city of Brighton and Hove and the surrounding area. As early as 1910 her mother, Augusta, gave her address as 71 Walsingham Road, Hove on her son Frank Dove's entry to Cranleigh School. On joining the army in 1916, Frank gave his home address as 71 Walsingham Road. After the war, in 1919, when he married Amelia Rawlinson, they gave their address as 2 Prince's Street, Brighton. The following month, on her marriage certificate, Evelyn gave her home address as 71 Walsingham Road, the same address given by her mother Augusta on her second marriage to Frederic Ram in 1929. When Augusta died in 1947 she was living at 21 Denmark Villas in Hove. Several wartime postcards in Evelyn's collection are from her mother, and they show The Old Manor House in Hurstpierpoint where Augusta and her husband were living at that time. A 1930s photograph has survived of Evelyn with her mother and step-father in the garden of the The Old Manor House. In the 1940s Evelyn made several appearances as a singer at Brighton's Grand Theatre. In 1953 she returned to Brighton to appear at the Theatre Royal in New Road in the play *Anna Lucasta*.

There are several sources that highlight Brighton and Hove's black history. These include two websites *Brighton and Hove Black History* (www.black-history.org.uk) and *Brighton and Hove Untold – The Untold Black and Asian History of Brighton and Hove* (www.bhuntold.co.uk). The latter is based on the many years of walking tours around the principal locations in the city centre by local historian Bert Williams MBE. There is also an entry for "Black Brighton" in Rose Collis's *The New Encyclopaedia of Brighton* (2010). Black historical figures who are included in these resources include Francis Barber (1735–1801), valet and secretary to Dr Samuel Johnson, who were frequent visitors to the home of Mrs Thrale of 78 West Street, Brighton; the violinist George Polgreen Bridgetower (1778–1860) who played in the Prince's band at the Royal Pavilion in Brighton for fourteen years; and Sarah Forbes Bonetta (1843–1880), Queen Victoria's West African goddaughter who, in 1862, married at St Nicholas' Church in Brighton.

One of the most celebrated black Victorians to be associated with Brighton was the African American Shakespearean actor Ira Aldridge (1807–

1867). Racism in America had prevented him from succeeding as an actor in that country, so most of his appearances were in Britain and on the continent. He gave his first known British performance in 1825 at London's Royal Coburg Theatre, later known as the Old Vic. However, racist press hostility in the midst of the controversy over the abolition of slavery made it difficult for Aldridge to establish himself in London at that time, so he pursued his acting career in the provinces. Aldridge acted in many plays, including Shakespeare's *Othello* and *Titus Andronicus* at Brighton's popular Theatre Royal during his thirty-year career on the British stage. In 1858, while appearing at Brighton's Theatre Royal, Aldridge responded to negative criticism from a local journalist:

I have struggled hard, encountering almost insurmountable difficulties, to make not only for myself, a name, but to refute the assertions made by the enemies of my race and colour, that we blacks are incapable of mental cultivation. I did not come to Brighton unsolicited. Mr Henry Nye Chart, a friend of long standing, gave me an invitation, which I accepted... When such an assertion is made in my presence, I unhesitatingly class the speaker as a false-speaking knave or fool.

There is now a chair at the Shakespeare Memorial Theatre in Stratford-upon-Avon dedicated to Aldridge's memory. In 2004 a framed print of Aldridge as Aaron in Shakespeare's *Titus Andronicus* was unveiled at the Old Vic. In *Ira Aldridge – The Negro Tragedian* (1958), Herbert Marshall and Mildred Stock described him as "The first to show that a black man could scale any heights in theatrical art reached by a white man—and recreate with equal artistry the greatest characters in world drama. He did this alone... on his own two feet, with his own skill, versatility and talent. He did this in a white world, and showed that if a white can blacken his skin to represent Othello, then a black man can whiten his skin to represent Lear, Macbeth, or Shylock with equal artistry."

Eddie Whaley was one half of an African American double act known as Scott and Whaley who began a long and successful career in British music halls in 1909. In 1933 they became nationally famous with their weekly appearances on BBC Radio in the popular series *Kentucky Minstrels*. Now and again they were featured in variety shows and on BBC Radio with Evelyn. The partnership ended in 1947 when Harry Scott died. Whaley made Brighton his family home in the 1930s and this is where his son, Eddie Whaley Jr, was born in 1939. During the war, when Harry Scott fell ill, Whaley and his young son, known as 'Little Whaley', became a double act. Whaley purchased 124 Marine Parade, next door to a house owned by the famous music hall entertainer Max Miller. He named it Whaley House and in the late 1940s and for most of the 1950s ran it as a hotel. It became a popular holiday home for entertainers and musicians, and among the black stars of British show business that visited Brighton and stayed at Whaley's hotel were Turner Layton, Leslie 'Hutch' Hutchinson, Ellis Jackson, Ray Ellington, Ike Hatch and Adelaide Hall. By 1960, however, Eddie Whaley Jr had moved to America, and Whaley himself moved to 27A Bear Road, Brighton. He died at that address on 13 November 1960 of heart failure. He was cremated at Brighton's Woodvale crematorium and his ashes were scattered in the garden of rest.

Appendix B: A Family Chronology of Births, Marriages and Deaths

Father: Francis Thomas Dove born 1869 in Freetown, Sierra Leone, West Africa. Son of William Thomas Dove and Mary Ann Dove, formerly Gerber.

Mother: Augusta Winchester born 3 March 1877 in Sandbanks, Hailsham, Sussex. Daughter of John Winchester, gardener and Louisa Winchester, formerly Edmonds.

Parent's marriage: 14 December 1896 at the Register Office in Marylebone, London.

Brother: Francis Sydney Dove born 3 September 1897 in City of London Lying-in Hospital, Holborn, London.

Second husband: Felix John Etherington Inglis Allen born 14 April 1909 at 27 Waldemar Avenue, Fulham, London.

Brother Frank's marriage: 26 August 1919 to Amelia Ethel Ellis Rawlinson at the Register Office in Brighton.

Evelyn's first marriage: 27 September 1919 to Milton Alphonso Luke at the Register Office in Lambeth, London.

Mother's second marriage: 16 April 1929 Augusta Dove to Frederic Montague Anson Ram at the Register Office, Steyning, Sussex.

Father's second marriage: 28 June 1929 Francis Dove to Nellie Elizabeth Brown at the Register Office, St. Marylebone, London.

Evelyn's second marriage: 19 March 1941 to Felix John Etherington Inglis Allen at the Register Office, Bristol.

Mother's death: 31 January 1947 Augusta Ram at Denmark Villas in Hove, East Sussex.

Father's death: 22 August 1949 Francis Dove at the Catholic Nursing Institute, 80 Lambeth Road in Southwark, London.

Brother's death: 10 February 1957 Francis Sydney Dove in Wolverhampton.

Evelyn's third marriage: 6 September 1958 to Willie Newton Brantley at the Register Office in St. Pancras, London.

Second husband's death: 5 June 1977 Felix Inglis Allen in St Bartholomews

Hospital, Smithfield, London.

Third husband's death: 14 May 1980 Willie Newton Brantley in Dade, Florida, USA.

Evelyn's death: 7 March 1987 in Horton Hospital, Epsom.

Appendix C:
Evelyn Dove's Credits

Theatre

1925 The Chocolate Kiddies (European tour)
1929 Brownbirds (British tour)
1945 Dick Whittington (Alexandra Theatre, Birmingham)
1948 Calypso (Wimbledon Theatre)
1951 London Melody (Empress Hall, Earl's Court)
1951 South Pacific (Theatre Royal, Drury Lane)
1953 Anna Lucasta (Theatre Royal, Brighton)
1954 Cry, the Beloved Country (St Martin-in-the-Fields)
1958 Simply Heavenly (Adelphi Theatre)
1961 A Wreath for Udomo (Lyric, Hammersmith)
1965 The Dark Disciples (tour)

Films

1921 British Pathé newsreel ("SS Rowan Survivors"), http://www.britishpathe.com/video/s-s-ss-rowan-survivors/query/SS
1957 The Story of Esther Costello

Television

1938 Picture Page (BBC)
1946–47 Serenade in Sepia (series) (BBC)
1947 Variety in Sepia (BBC)
1948 Sepia (BBC)
1951 Kaleidoscope (BBC)
1951 Sunday-Night Theatre: London Melody (BBC)
1954 Sunday-Night Theatre: Halcyon Days (BBC)
1954 Music for You (BBC)
1955 Meet the Commonwealth (BBC)
1956 Sunday-Night Theatre: Mrs Patterson (BBC)
1957 Another Part of the Forest (ITV)
1958 Sunday-Night Theatre: The Green Pastures (BBC)
Note: Copies of Mrs Patterson and The Green Pastures are held in the BFI National Archive (http://www.bfi.org.uk/archive-collections)

BBC Radio

1925
Negro Melodies (London)
Independence Day (London)
Way Down South (London)

1939
Monday Night at Seven (National)
Mississippi Nights (National)
Sweet and Lovely (series) (Home Service)

1940

Dance Cabaret (from the Grand Hotel, Torquay) (Home Service)

Honolulu Beach (Home Service)

Non-Stop Express (For the Forces)

Cabaret (from the Polygon Hotel, Southampton) (Home Service)

Rhapsody in Black (series) (Home Service and For the Forces)

Bill for Lunch (For the Forces)

Felix Mendelsohnn's Hawaiian Serenaders (For the Forces)

A Smile and a Song (series) (Home Service)

Plantation Songs (series) (For the Forces)

Cabaret-Variety (For the Forces)

Theatreland (Home Service)

Variety (For the Forces)

1941

Sunday Matinee (For the Forces)

Sweetness Itself (For the Forces)

Mint Julep (series) (Home Service)

Cabaret (For the Forces)

Country Hotel Cabaret (For the Forces)

Fresh Airs (series) (Home Service)

Repeat Refrain (Home Service)

The Land Where the Good Songs Go (For the Forces)

Negro Spirituals (For the Forces)

Grin and It (Home Service)

Evelyn Dove (series)(Home Service)

1942

Starlight (For the Forces)

The Whoopee Club (For the Forces)

At Home to the Forces (series) (For the Forces)

Songs for Everybody (Home Service)

Plantation Songs and Spirituals (For the Forces)

1944

The Dansant (series) (Home Service)

Bandstand (General Forces)

Spotlight (series) (General Forces)

£250 Red Cross Radio Contest (Home Service)

Grand Hotel (series) (General Forces)

Modern Light Music of America (General Forces)

1945

Round the World in Song (series) (Home Service and Light Programme)

Over to You (General Forces)

Serenade in Sepia (series) (Home Service and Light Programme)

Variety Bandbox (series) (General Forces)

Break for Music (Home Service)

Atlantic Spotlight (General Forces)

British Band of the A. E. F. (General Forces)

Easy to Remember (Home Service)

Journey to Romance (Light Programme)

1946

Dick Whittington (from the Alexandra Theatre, Birmingham) (Light Programme)

BBC Midland Light Orchestra (Light Programme)

Music from the Movies (series) (Light Programme)

Cabaret (from the Branksome Tower Hotel, Bournemouth) (Light Programme)
Song of the South (Home Service)

1947
Rainbow Room (Light Programme)
Tea-Time Variety (Light Programme)
Breakfast Hour (series) (Light Programme)
Mood in Ebony (series) (Light Programme)
Variety Concert Hall (from the Embassy Cinema, Bristol) (Light Programme)
Variety Bandbox (from the People's Palace, London) (Light Programme)

1948
Workers Playtime (Light Programme)

1951
Variety Bandbox (Light Programme)
Rendevous (Light Programme)
Henry Hall's Guest Night (Light Programme)

Discography

1924 *Couldn't Hear Nobody Pray*
1924 *Ev'ry Time I Feel the Spirit*

Singles (78 rpm)
1939–40
My Heart Belongs to Daddy with Billy Cotton and his Band. Recorded on 27 October 1939 (Rex 9667)

Side A: *I'll Pray For You*/Side B: *Over the Rainbow* with Instrumental Accompaniment (Rex 9722)

Gulliver's Travels – Film Selection. Part 2 includes "We're All Together Now" (instrumental) and Evelyn's version of "I Hear a Dream" with Louis Levy and His Orchestra. Recorded in December 1939 (Columbia FB2346)

Babes in Arms – Film Selection. Part 2 includes "The Lady is a Tramp" (instrumental) and Evelyn's version of "Where or When" with Louis Levy and His Orchestra. Recorded in January 1940 (Columbia FB2368)

Band Wagon – Film Selection. Part 1 includes "Band Wagon" (instrumental) and Evelyn's version of "Heaven Will Be Heavenly" with Louis Levy and His Orchestra. Recorded in 1940 (Columbia FB2380)

Compact Discs

'Brother Can You Spare a Dime?' – The Roots of American Song (Pearl, 1991) includes Evelyn's recordings of "Couldn't Hear Nobody Pray" and "Ev'ry Time I Feel the Spirit".

"My Heart Belongs to Daddy" has been reissued on the CD compilation *The Great British Dance Bands* (Past Perfect, 1994), compiled by Hugh Palmer.

'Babes in Arms – Film Selection' including Evelyn's version of "Where or When" has been reissued on the CD compilation *Music From the Movies – The Thirties: Louis Levy and his Gaumont British Symphony* (Living Era, 2002).

Appendix D: Salutations

A BBC Radio 2 series compiled and researched by Stephen Bourne

In 1993 *Salutations* was broadcast for nine weeks, every Saturday from 11 September to 6 November, at 7pm on BBC Radio 2. The idea came from me when I was asked to submit ideas for programmes to Ladbroke Radio for broadcasting on Radio 2. The series was presented by Moira Stuart and it was scripted and produced by Jim Hiley.

Salutations celebrated the lives and music of African, Caribbean and black British singers, entertainers and musicians who had been part of Britain's musical landscape from the 1930s to the 1950s. Archive material was interspersed with recent interviews with the artistes' friends and colleagues, including Adelaide Hall and Elisabeth Welch. The series focused on Leslie 'Hutch' Hutchinson, Reginald Foresythe, Evelyn Dove, Leslie 'Jiver' Hutchinson, Leslie Thompson, Ken 'Snakehips' Johnson, Rudolph Dunbar, Fela Sowande, Cyril Blake, Edric Connor, Winifred Atwell, Ray Ellington, Cy Grant, Geoff Love and Shirley Bassey.

The series was well-received and Jim Hiley and myself were nominated for the Commission for Racial Equality's *Race in the Media* award for Best Radio Current Affairs/Documentary. On 12 April 1994, at the grand awards ceremony at The Hyatt Carlton Tower in Cadogan Place (off Sloane Street), Jim and I won the award, which was a wonderful surprise. It was presented to us by the actor Rudolph Walker. Jim said: "It is wonderful for us, as an independent company, to win for a programme for Radio 2. I am delighted that it highlights the range and diversity of programmes on the network."

Note: Evelyn's story was told in the second half of Programme 2 of the *Salutations* series, broadcast on 18 September. The first half of the programme focused on the innovative jazz composer Reginald Foresythe (1907–1958), who was also born in London to a West African father and an English mother. Some the information in Evelyn's *Salutations* broadcast is incorrect. Further research has revealed that Evelyn and Adelaide Hall left the cast of *The Chocolate Kiddies* revue before it was seen by Joseph Stalin in Russia in 1926.

RADIO 2 JINGLE *"It's all for you, Radio 2!"*

15. MOIRA:

"This is Moira Stuart and you're listening to SALUTATIONS on BBC Radio 2, the series that celebrates black British, African and Caribbean entertainers from the 1930s to the 1950s. And like Reginald Foresythe, Evelyn Dove hardly had the recognition she deserved towards the end of her career, but at its height she was immensely popular, not least broadcasting to the troops during World War Two. Evelyn Dove was an inspirational singer in every sense as you can hear from this recording made as long ago as 1926."

16. MUSIC – EV'RY TIME I FEEL THE SPIRIT

17. MOIRA:

"EV'RY TIME I FEEL THE SPIRIT sung by Evelyn Dove, a graduate of the Royal Academy of Music and she was surely one of Britain's most versatile singing stars this century—equally at home with sentimental ballads and throbbing torch songs. Evelyn Dove's background was highly respectable. Her mother was English, and her father, another similarity with Reginald Foresythe, was West African. Jeffrey Green has looked back into Evelyn Dove's rather privileged family tree."

18. (i) TAPE – JEFFREY GREEN

"Evelyn Dove's grandfather had made a fortune in trading from out of Freetown, Sierra Leone into the interior and thousands of miles along the coast beyond Nigeria. His children were educated in England. Evelyn Dove's father was a barrister. Her uncle was a barrister. They had trading investments. They spent more of their time in Europe than they did in Africa. It was natural that the Doves married English women and it was natural also that their children were brought up in Britain. It may be a surprise for listeners to find out that there were many middle-class Africans who were more at home in England at the turn of this century than they were in West Africa."

(ii) MUSIC – OVER THE RAINBOW

(iii) TAPE – JEFFREY GREEN

"Evelyn Dove had a brother Frank who went to Oxford University. Evelyn herself studied at the Royal Academy of Music and she took tuition with some of London's leading voice coaches. Symbolic of the Dove's role in African British life in the 1910s is the fact that whilst Evelyn Dove was at the Royal Academy of Music, her brother was being awarded the Military Medal for driving a tank at the first tank battle in Cambrai in 1917 on the Western Front. He was, like so many British males, fighting for King and Country."

(iv) MUSIC – OVER THE RAINBOW

(v) TAPE – JEFFREY GREEN

"She was an extremely beautiful

woman. Everybody, almost everybody knows of Josephine Baker. Evelyn Dove was likened to Josephine Baker."

(vi) MUSIC – OVER THE RAINBOW

19. MOIRA:

"For a black singer of Evelyn Dove's generation, the world of jazz was far more welcoming than the concert hall that she had trained for. So too were the all-black jazz revues that had mushroomed in America during the Harlem renaissance, and were soon being recreated in Europe. One such was CHOCOLATE KIDDIES in 1925, and its star was Adelaide Hall."

20. (i) TAPE – ADELAIDE HALL

"She was a really lovely girl and a very smart looking girl. And she sang 'Jericho'. I think Evelyn was English, born in this country and she joined up with our company. She joined the cast of *Chocolate Kiddies* and we travelled all through Europe. Germany. I think Vienna. Budapest."

(ii) MUSIC – WHERE OR WHEN

(iii) TAPE – ADELAIDE HALL

"I remember Evelyn sang well and looked good. Looked very good."

(iv) MUSIC – WHERE OR WHEN

21. MOIRA:

"CHOCOLATE KIDDIES toured Western Europe for a year, then headed east. And in the audience one night in Moscow, Evelyn Dove and Adelaide Hall were being watched by a perhaps unlikely jazz freak, one Joseph Stalin. Back in Britain, Harlem-type revue remained for a while the mainstay of Dove's career."

22. TAPE – JEFFREY GREEN

"A black American named Will Garland had lived in England from the earlier part of the twentieth century and he ran all-black shows. He toured thousands of miles across Europe. He employed Africans, he employed West Indians and of course he employed people like Evelyn Dove who were born of African parents in Britain. The New York *Blackbirds* shows came to Britain in the 1920s. Will Garland copied them as *Brownbirds*. Evelyn Dove starred in the Will Garland *Brownbirds* shows as well as appearing on the radio."

23. MOIRA:

"And it was through radio that her career approached its peak. Her wartime performances for the troops enjoyed similar appeal to Vera Lynn's, as did her special broadcasts to the Caribbean. Later, she starred in the long-running radio series, SERENADE IN SEPIA, and it was such a hit that it was quickly moved to television. By the way her co-star in that ground-breaking series, Edric Connor, will be profiled in a later edition of SALUTATIONS. Now though here's Evelyn Dove recorded at the height of her fame."

24. MUSIC – I'LL PRAY FOR YOU

25. MOIRA:

"Evelyn Dove with I'LL PRAY FOR YOU. By the 1950s engagements were few and far between. So drastic was the decline that the BBC was asked to provide a reference when she applied for work as a telephone operator. But she returned for occasional acting jobs, and here's a rare chance to hear her in those later days of her career.

In 1956, she appeared live on BBC Television in MRS PATTERSON, a Sunday night drama vehicle for Eartha Kitt. Eartha plays a girl in the Deep South who's obsessed by her mother's rich white employer. Her mother was played by Evelyn Dove."

26. TAPE – MRS PATTERSON

27. MOIRA:

"The once-renowned singing star—who'd sung before Stalin with Adelaide Hall—in what was clearly now a supporting role. Evelyn Dove became ill in the 1960s, and was admitted to a nursing home. She died in 1987, at the age of 85. But however unhappy the end of her life, and however few the recordings she left behind, it's still impossible not to be inspired by her voice.

In the third edition of SALUTATIONS the jazz musicians who inspired the nation in wartime. Remember Leslie Thompson? 'Jiver' Hutchinson? And the Ken 'Snakehips' Johnson band? Hope you'll join me Moira Stuart to hear them all next week.

SALUTATIONS is compiled and researched by Stephen Bourne, written and produced by Jim Hiley, and is a Ladbroke Radio production for BBC Radio 2. For now though I'll leave you now with the late, great Evelyn Dove."

28. MUSIC – EV'RY TIME I FEEL THE SPIRIT

Further Reading

Albertson, Chris, *Bessie – Empress of the Blues* (Abacus, 1975)

Banham, Martin, Hill, Errol and Woodyard, George, *The Cambridge Guide to African and Caribbean Theatre* (Cambridge University Press, 1994)

Behncke, Bernard H., 'Sam Wooding and the Chocolate Kiddies in Hamburg 1925', *Storyville*, No. 60 (August-September 1975): 214–21

Bourne, Stephen, 'Eartha Kitt – One of a Kind', *Films and Filming* (September, 1989)

Bourne, Stephen, 'Highflying Spirit of a Dove', *The Weekly Journal* (1 October 1992)

Bourne, Stephen, 'Spirit of a Dove' (Evelyn Dove), *Pride* (July, 1999)

Bourne, Stephen, *Sophisticated Lady – A Celebration of Adelaide Hall* (Ethnic Communities Oral History Project, 2001)

Bourne, Stephen, *Black in the British Frame – The Black Experience in British Film and Television* (Continuum, 2001)

Bourne, Stephen, 'Dove, Evelyn Mary (1902–1987)', *Oxford Dictionary of National Biography* (Oxford University Press, 2004)

Bourne, Stephen, 'Connor, Edric Esclus (1913–1968)', *Oxford Dictionary of National Biography* (Oxford University Press, 2004)

Bourne, Stephen, 'Hall, Adelaide Louise Estelle (1901–1993)', *Oxford Dictionary of National Biography* (Oxford University Press, 2004)

Bourne, Stephen, 'Lucas, Isabelle Harriet (1927–1997)', *Oxford Dictionary of National Biography* (Oxford University Press, 2004)

Bourne, Stephen, 'Welch, Elisabeth Margaret (1904–2003)', *Oxford Dictionary of National Biography* (Oxford University Press, 2004)

Bourne, Stephen, *Elisabeth Welch – Soft Lights and Sweet Music* (Scarecrow Press, 2005)

Bourne, Stephen, 'Josie Woods: Tap-dancing star of music hall' (obituary), *The Independent* (23 August 2008)

Brown, Jayna, *Babylon Girls – Black Women Performers and the Shaping of the Modern* (Duke University Press, 2008)

Bushell, Garvin (with Mark Tucker), *Jazz from the Beginning* (Bayou Press, 1988)

Cameron Williams, Iain, *Underneath a Harlem Moon – The Harlem to Paris Years of Adelaide Hall* (Continuum, 2002)

Chambers, Colin, *Black and Asian Theatre in Britain – A History* (Routledge, 2011)

Chilton, John, *Who's Who of Jazz – Storyville to Swing Street* (Papermac, 1989)

Chilton, John, *Who's Who of British Jazz* (Cassell, 1997)

Clarke, Donald, *Wishing on the Moon – The Life and Times of Billie Holiday* (Viking, 1994)

Connor, Edric, *Horizons – The Life and*

Times of Edric Connor 1913–1968 (Ian Randle Publishers, 2007)

Deffaa, Chip, *Voices of the Jazz Age – Profiles of Eight Vintage Jazzmen* (Bayou Press, 1990)

Doffman, Mark, Tackley, Catherine and Toynbee, Jason (eds.), *Black British Jazz – Routes, Ownership and Performance* (Ashgate, 2014)

Englund, Bjorn, 'Chocolate Kiddies – The Show That Brought Jazz to Europe and Russia in 1925', *Storyville* No. 62 (December 1975–January 1976): 44–50

Egan, Bill, *Florence Mills – Harlem Jazz Queen* (Scarecrow Press, 2004)

Gadzekpo, Audrey and Newell, Stephanie (eds.), *Mabel Dove – Selected Writings of a Pioneer West African Feminist* (Trent Editions, 2004)

Green, Jeffrey, 'High Society and Black Entertainers in the 1920s and 1930s', *New Community* (Spring 1987)

Green, Jeffrey, 'The Negro Renaissance in England,' in Samuel A. Floyd Jr., (ed.) *Black Music in the Harlem Renaissance* (Greenwood Press, 1990)

Green, Jeffrey, *Black Edwardians – Black People in Britain 1901–1914* (Frank Cass, 1998)

Green, Jeffrey and Lotz, Rainer E., 'Davis, Belle (1874–in or after 1938),' *Oxford Dictionary of National Biography* (Oxford University Press, 2004)

Green, Jeffrey and Lotz, Rainer E., 'Garland, Will (1878–1938),' *Oxford Dictionary of National Biography* (Oxford University Press, 2004)

Green, Jeffrey, Lotz, Rainer E. and Rye, Howard, *Black Europe* (Bear Records, 2013)

Greer, Bonnie, *A Parallel Life* (Arcadia Books, 2014)

Hammond, Bryan and O'Connor, Patrick, *Josephine Baker* (Jonathan Cape, 1988)

Harris, Roxie and White, Sarah (eds.), *Changing Britannia – Life Experience With Britain* (New Beacon Books, 1999)

Haskins, Jim, *The Cotton Club* (Robson Books, 1985)

Hatch, James V. and Hill, Errol G., *A History of African American Theatre* (Cambridge University Press, 2003)

Hughes, Langston, *The Big Sea* (Knopf, 1940)

Johnson, James Weldon, *Black Manhattan* (Knopf, 1930)

Kitt, Eartha, *I'm Still Here* (Sidgwick and Jackson, 1989)

Lotz, Rainer E. And Pegg, Ian (eds.), *Under the Imperial Carpet – Essays in*

Black History 1780–1950 (Rabbit Press, 1986)

Lotz, Rainer E., *Black People – Entertainers of African Descent in Europe, and Germany* (Birgit Lotz Verlag, 1997)

Nettles, Darryl Glenn, *African American Concert Singers Before 1950* (McFarland, 2003)

Newton, Darrell M., *Paving the Empire Road – BBC Television and Black Britons* (Manchester University Press, 2011)

Oliver, Paul (ed.), *Black Music in Britain – Essays on the Afro-Asian Contribution to Popular Music* (Open University Press, 1990)

Peterson, Jr., Bernard L., *A Century of Musicals in Black and White – An Encyclopedia of Musical Stage Works By, About, or Involving African Americans* (Greenwood Press, 1993)

Pines, Jim (ed.), *Black and White in Colour – Black People in British Television since 1936* (British Film Institute, 1992) includes Stephen Bourne's interviews with Elisabeth Welch and Pearl Connor.

Rye, Howard., 'Showgirls and Stars: Black-Cast Revues and Female Performers in Britain 1903-1939', *Popular Music History*, 1/2 (2006): 167–88

Sampson, Henry T., *Blacks in Blackface – A Source Book on Early Black Musical Shows* (Scarecrow Press, 1980)

Shack, William A., *Harlem in Montmartre – A Paris Jazz Story Between the Great Wars* (University of California Press, 2001)

Shaw, Arnold, *The Jazz Age – Popular Music in the 1920s* (Oxford University Press, 1987)

Singer, Barry, *Black and Blue – The Life and Lyrics of Andy Razaf* (Schirmer Books, 1992)

Stearns, Marshall and Jean, *Jazz Dance – The Story of American Vernacular Dance* (Da Capo Press, 1994)

Thompson, Leslie (with Jeffrey Green), *Swing from a Small Island – The Story of Leslie Thompson* (Northway Publications, 2009)

Vail, Ken, *Lady Day's Diary – The Life of Billie Holiday 1937–1959* (Castle Communications, 1996)

Walmsley, Anne, *The Caribbean Artists Movement 1966–1972* (New Beacon Books, 1992)

Williams, John L., *America's Mistress – The Life and Times of Eartha Kitt* Quercus, 2013)

Woll, Allen, *Black Musical Theatre – From Coontown to Dreamgirls* (Louisiana State University Press, 1989)

About the Author

Stephen Bourne is a writer, film and social historian specialising in black culture. As noted by the BBC among others, Stephen "has discovered many stories that have remained untold for years." Bonnie Greer, the acclaimed playwright and critic, says: "Stephen brings great natural scholarship and passion to a largely hidden story. His is highly accessible, accurate and surprising. You always walk away from his work knowing something that you didn't know, that you didn't even expect."

Stephen was born in Camberwell, South-East London and raised in Peckham. He graduated from the London College of Printing with a Bachelor's degree in film and television in 1988, and in 2006 received a Master's of Philosophy degree at De Montfort University on the subject of the representation of gay men in British television drama 1936–1979.

After graduating in 1988, he was a research officer at the British Film Institute on a project that documented the history of black people in British television. The result was a two-part television documentary called *Black and White in Colour* (BBC 1992), directed by Isaac Julien, that is considered ground-breaking. In 1991

Stephen was a founder member of the Black and Asian Studies Association. In 1999 he undertook pioneering work with Southwark Council and the Metropolitan Police as a voluntary independent adviser to the police.

In 2008 he researched *Keep Smiling Through – Black Londoners on the Home Front 1939–1945*, an exhibition for the Cuming Museum in the London Borough of Southwark and that same year he worked as a historical consultant on the Imperial War Museum's *War to Windrush* exhibition.

In 1991, Stephen co-authored *Aunt Esther's Story* with Esther Bruce (his adopted aunt), which was published by Hammersmith and Fulham's

Ethnic Communities Oral History Project. Nancy Daniels in *The Voice* (8 October 1991) described the book as "Poignantly and simply told, the story of Aunt Esther is a factual account of a black working-class woman born in turn of the century London. The book is a captivating documentation of a life rich in experiences, enhanced by good black and white photographs." For *Aunt Esther's Story*, Stephen and Esther were shortlisted for the 1992 Raymond Williams Prize for Community Publishing.

In 2002 Stephen received the Metropolitan Police Volunteer Award "in recognition of dedicated service and commitment to supporting the Metropolitan Police in Southwark." It was presented to him by Police Commissioner Sir John Stevens and Mayor of London Ken Livingstone at City Hall, London. In 2013 Stephen was nominated for a Southwark Heritage blue plaque for his work as a community historian and Southwark Police independent adviser. He came second with 1,025 votes.

In 2014, Stephen's book *Black Poppies – Britain's Black Community and the Great War* was published by The History Press to coincide with the centenary of Britain's entry into the First World War. Reviewing it in *The Independent* (11 September 2014), Bernadine Evaristo said: "Until historians and cultural map-makers stop ignoring the historical presence of people of colour, books such as this provide a powerful, revelatory counterbalance to the whitewashing of British history." For *Black Poppies* Stephen received the 2015 Southwark Arts Forum Literature Award at Southwark's Unicorn Theatre.

Selected publications

Aunt Esther's Story (ECOHP, 1991)
Brief Encounters (Cassell, 1996)
Black in the British Frame – The Black Experience in British Film and Television (Cassell/Continuum, 2001)
Sophisticated Lady – A Celebration of Adelaide Hall (ECOHP, 2001)
Elisabeth Welch – Soft Lights and Sweet Music (Scarecrow Press, 2005)
Speak of Me As I Am – The Black Presence in Southwark Since 1600 (Southwark Council, 2005)
Ethel Waters – Stormy Weather (Scarecrow Press, 2007)
Dr. Harold Moody (Southwark Council, 2008)
Mother Country – Britain's Black Community on the Home Front 1939–45 (The History Press, 2010)
The Motherland Calls – Britain's Black Servicemen and Women 1939–45 (The History Press, 2012)
Black Poppies – Britain's Black Community and the Great War (The History Press, 2014)

For further information go to www.stephenbourne.co.uk

Index